THE TRIANGULATION OF SUCCESS

SECRETS TO MULTI-ORGANIZATION SUCCESSES

DR. TIMOTHY LOW

PRABHAT PAPERBACKS

Published by
PRABHAT PAPERBACKS
An imprint of Prabhat Prakashan Pvt. Ltd.
4/19 Asaf Ali Road,
New Delhi-110 002 (INDIA)
e-mail: prabhatbooks@gmail.com

ISBN 978-93-5521-490-4
THE TRIANGULATION OF SUCCESS
Secrets To Multi-Organization Successes
by Dr. Timothy Low

Edition
First, 2023

Price
₹ 300 (Rupees Three Hundred Only)

Printed at
Japan Art, Delhi

To all leaders - then, now and forever.

May you touch the people you lead, empower them by making a difference in their lives.

"The art of giving fine service can only be mastered through actual practice. Timothy Low is a long-time practitioner of this fine art and, in this book, clearly communicates how it is done. Read it. Then do it."

– Professor Maurice Choo

Chairman, The Farrer Park Company

Adjunct Professor, Lee Kong Chian School of Medicine

"Dr. Timothy Low's book highlights how to be a CEO, a leader that the employees will look up to and follow when growing the business. This book also emphasizes service, service, and service, which is so relevant in the hospitality business, be it in the F&B, healthcare, hotel, or airline industries. I would recommend all service captains to read this book and remember the incidents mentioned so as not to repeat them again, and to avoid similar situations. My congratulations to Dr. Low for coming out with this book, which will benefit everyone in the service industry."

– Dr. Lim Cheok Peng

Chairman, Putra Group of Hospitals and Kidney Dialysis Foundation

Former CEO, Parkway Holdings and Managing Director, IHH Healthcare

"In this book, Timothy shows his experience and dedication to organization building and excellence. It contains a wealth of knowledge for practitioners in healthcare and beyond in

their pursuit to build better teams and organizations. A must read to improve ourselves."

– Tow Heng Tan

CEO, Pavilion Capital International

Former Chief Investment Officer, Temasek Holdings

"Dr. Timothy Low led the transformation of two of Singapore's major hospitals from ordinary places to award-winning hospitals—known far and wide for both superior patient outcomes and excellent service to the patients, their families, and the community. The Triangulation of Success provides numerous practical recommendations and examples so other executives can do the same at their organizations."

– Professor David Ahlstrom

Professor of Department of Management

The Chinese University of Hong Kong (CUHK) Business School

"When (Timothy) Tim and I were working together, one of the things that most impressed me was his kindness. Being a seasoned leader with a strong idea of where he wants to go, he never went anywhere without making sure that he could motivate people to follow him on his way. Tim truly and deeply cares about the individual, and this also is an essential message of his wonderful book. It explains how you can become a leader who does his magic by caring, encouraging innovation, and listening to the needs of both customers and employees. The examples Tim provides in his book show how we all can learn from each other to become the best and most successful leader we can be."

– Dr. Martina Muttke

Mentor, Adviser, and Speaker

Former Head Medical International, SHIRE

"If a leader writes from his heart and from his own practice, sharing the story of getting meaningful results for the people outside and inside the organization (and not forgetting the realistic profitability), it is mostly worth reading and so is Timothy's authentic discourse of years being there. The consistency throughout this book is energizing and motivating, and makes hard-to-find leadership lessons extremely accessible. The models he uses are nice and solid, but the values behind his work are the core of everything that is conveyed."

– Professor Peter Robertson

Psychiatrist, Creator of AEM-Cube, and Executive Lecturer
Visiting Research Fellow at Nyenrode Business University

"I have had the privilege of working with Tim for more than two decades. What he captured in the Triangulation of Success was the customer's satisfaction journey with companies that sell services or products, which he argues well with many illustrations and anecdotes. In my view, the Triangulation of Success comes with practical pointers on how to generate the 'wow experience' within the triangle of engagement of employer, employee and customer. Tim's experience as a service mogul has won him many accolades and recognition — it boils down to how much he cares."

– Dr. Stephen Phua

Chairman, Menarini Biomarkers
Board Member, Zuellig Pharma

"Tim Low has synthesized the learnings from a number of corporate successes and failures and applied this knowledge to his own management of a large hospital

group in Singapore with very successful results. This book serves as an excellent reminder that we can always learn from unrelated and diverse companies and use that knowledge to benefit our own business."

– Dr. F. John Mills

Former Chairman and CEO of BioStorage Technologies Inc
United States of America

"The Triangulation of Success reminds us that inspiring leadership begins with empathy. Dr. Timothy reveals some excellent insights into how to connect and communicate with your employees."

– Mukul Deva

Internationally Bestselling Author of the Lashkar and Ravinder Gill series
Founder of Influence Solutions and MSD Security

"Great real-life scenarios and insights on how Dr. Low developed a resilient, flexible, growth-oriented, visionary, and holistic mindset from both employees' and patients' perspectives. Ultimately, his approach has successfully adapted to situations that positively impacted the hospital culture. I strongly recommend Dr. Low's book for anyone seeking proven strategies to strengthen their teams, transform organizational culture, and maximize performance."

– Dr. Robert Edmonson

C-Suite Executive Coach and Leadership Author
Paradigm 21 Group

Author's Note

Some twenty years ago, as a young keen-eyed student, I was taught one leadership lesson that I would never forget to this day.

During my final year at medical school, our professor gave us a pop quiz. As a conscientious student, I breezed through the questions, until I read the last one:

"What is the first name of the woman who cleans the school?"

I frowned hard at the words. Surely this was some kind of joke.

I had seen the cleaning woman several times. She was tall, with silver hair, and in her late 50s, but how would I know her name?

I handed in my paper, leaving the last question blank. Just before class ended, a student asked if the last question would count towards our grade.

"Absolutely," said the professor. "In your career, you will meet many people.

All are significant.

They deserve your attention and care, even if all you do is smile and say'hello'."

I've never forgotten that lesson. I've also never forgotten that her name was Aunty Lucy.

Today, leaders across the world are in desperate need of such lessons.

Facing the predicament of geopolitical crises and the unprecedented threat of a global virus, we are clearly in a VUCA world (volatility, uncertainty, complexity, and ambiguity).

Even after this virus has abated, we wll still be in uncertain times due to weakening in the economy. It is in such times that the solution is to be caring and empathetic to the needs of the people around us.

Customers, employees, vendors, management, and shareholders they are all people who need our care and empathy in order for all of us to not just survive, but to thrive.

Like any crisis, it can lead to a breakdown or a breakthrough.

In order to breakthrough, as leaders, we need to focus on shifting our people out of this crisis by creating a new possibility for everone.

I propose that we begin with 'HEN' in mind.

H - Habits

E - Expectations

N - Needs

Throughout the pages you are about to read, you wll see these attributes consistently play out in various scenarios.

As a leader in your career, the way you treat people makes all the difference between imminent failure and great success.

This book is a guide and holds the leadership lessons I learned in my journey of leading and growing organizations from stagnancy to multimillion dollar successes.

– Dr. Timothy Low

Contents

CHAPTER 1 ▶▶▸

"Conventional Wisdom"

All passengers were buckled up and ready to fly on Flight 3411, but just before takeoff, an airline supervisor boarded the plane, announcing that United Airlines employees were required to join this flight and they were not taking off till four passengers gave up their seats.

In exchange, they offered $400 in United vouchers, including a hotel stay and a replacement flight scheduled to take off 21 hours later. When no one volunteered, the offer was doubled to $800 in vouchers—which also saw zero takers.

When it was clear that none of the passengers were willing to deplane, the United staff told everyone that four passengers would be selected randomly by a computer.

Four names were drawn and three passengers agreed to deplane. But not 69-year-old Dr. David Dao, a pulmonary doctor who specializes in lung health. He refused, stating that his presence was required at the hospital the following morning.

The airline supervisor promptly called the airport security, and three officers entered Flight 3411. After a heated exchange, the officers unbuckled and forcibly yanked the struggling doctor out of his seat, slamming his head against a metal armrest in the process.

Knocked unconscious and bleeding heavily from the mouth, Dr. David Dao was dragged by his hands to the exit of the plane. He suffered a concussion, a broken nose, and lost his front two teeth during the scuffle.

The ordeal was filmed by other passengers, with one video shared approximately 87,000 times and viewed as many as 6.8 million times in less than 24 hours—leading to a major backlash on United Airlines across social media platforms.

United Airlines' shares fell 6.3 per cent, dropping as much as $1.4 billion dollars.

When You Only Serve Your Own Agenda

One of the critical errors with businesses today is that most people are just concerned about themselves.

Or, as we will explore further, the fault also lies in employees following instructions unthinkingly. The desire to perform tasks without the weight of responsibility and reasoning can be more powerful, often more so than conscious self-serving behaviour.

From the ground staff to the middle management to the C-level executives—it is the same self-serving tendency that has led to disasters such as the United Airlines Flight 3411 scandal.

The United Airlines supervisor was simply carrying out instructions. And the airport security officers were following procedures.

Perhaps they were concerned about protecting their jobs—nothing wrong with that. But clearly, not one of them was thinking about their customers.

"An airline supervisor walked onto the plane and brusquely announced: 'We have United employees that need to fly to

Louisville tonight. This flight's not leaving till four people get off,'", Tyler Bridges, said in a CNN interview after the incident.

Another passenger, Jason Powell, agrees with Bridges, saying that he was taken aback and surprised by the supervisor's annoyed and hostile tone, which immediately *turned him off*, and that "she accelerated the situation. It was poor leadership."

Mary Myers, who had also boarded the plane, commented, "I really put all this on (the supervisor's) shoulders. She could have made a difference. She could have handled it differently. She's the one who started it all."

These statements from Flight 3411 passengers beg the question: if the airline supervisor considered the feelings of her passengers first and broached the subject factfully, would things have happened very differently?

Of course, there is no guarantee that four passengers would voluntarily relinquish their seats when asked courteously. But based on the comments from the passengers, the airline supervisor's attitude likely played a critical factor in gluing passengers to their seats.

Force, After All, Always Begets Resistance.

What we can conclude, however, is that with a customer-centric and service-focused attitude, this incident would never have happened.

Most profitable companies in the world abide by this simple but elusive "service excellence" model. Companies renowned for the way they treat their employees and customers are also multi-million or billion-dollar empires, and it is no coincidence that the two are linked.

Companies that don't prioritize service excellence tend to face scandals that hurt their reputation, affecting their sales and revenue. Many such businesses also end up fighting multiple lawsuits each year, which costs hundreds of millions of dollars in settlements.

They are simply not aware of how their approach to service massively affects their bottom line.

We will be exploring these issues together throughout this book.

An Airline with a Heart

Since we are on the topic of airlines, let us take a comparative look at Southwest Airlines from the United States.

You might have noticed that they have rebranded themselves as Southwest Heart. Their mission and values are based on love for their customers.

Their slogan says it all:

"You are not a seat number to us — you are a person."

Surprisingly, this "love customers attitude" runs counter to the practices of many other airlines. Today's airline industry is rife with overbooked flights and an unapproachable attitude to passengers. In the case of United Airlines, their passenger Dr. Dao was just an unimportant seat number that needed to be replaced.

Southwest cares for every passenger.

In Return, They Gained the Trust and Loyalty of Every Passenger.

It sounds simple, but the differences between the service levels of Southwest and United Airlines are on completely opposite ends of the scale. In the difficult days following the September 11 attacks where planes were grounded and many frequent flight cancellations occurred, it showed us the true mettle of different airlines.

People were fearful of boarding a plane and the airline as an industry was taking a nosedive—no pun intended.

During these grim circumstances, Southwest had to make critical decisions, especially regarding cancellations and refunds that could make or break the company. The CEO of Southwest Airlines at the time was James F. Parker, who had only taken office a few months earlier.

"We didn't have time to do an economic analysis to figure out what the effects would be," Parker said. "We just had to go with our gut based on what we thought was important."

Southwest decided to offer refunds to customers freely upon request, without any confusing terms and conditions stipulated in the fine print. It was a nerve-wracking choice to make because an influx of refunds could bankrupt the airline.

At the time, airlines didn't even know when they could return to the skies... or if they would be allowed to fly again at all.

But it turned out that customers did not want refunds from Southwest.

Many were happy to hold on to credit for a future flight. Many people sent letters containing best wishes and even donations to Southwest in the wake of 9/11, in the hope of helping the airline weather the storm.

They were returning the favour for the excellent service rendered from Southwest employees in the past.

Here's a case study of Southwest's legendary customer service: an elderly passenger was scheduled to meet her son who was driving from Tucson, Arizona to receive her in Phoenix.

En route, he was caught in a traffic accident and was grievously hurt.

On landing in Phoenix, a Southwest employee tried to connect her to another airline to get her to Tucson but was unable to find a flight for her.

Despite running out of options, this plucky employee didn't give up. He didn't even call Southwest HQ and ask for help. Instead, he simply got into his car and drove this lady all the way to Tucson. It was a 100-mile drive.

Following the 9/11 disaster, Southwest did what other airlines could not—they did not lay off employees or reduce their salaries. They even honoured a nine-figure contribution to an employee profit-sharing plan, which amounted to $179 million dollars.

In the fourth quarter of 2001, Southwest reported positive cash flow. In the consecutive years since they were founded, they have always managed to turn a profit. They were unfettered by disasters like 9/11 or the oil crises of the 1970s or the early 2000s.

To date, Southwest Airlines remains the most profitable airline in history. Coincidence? The evidence suggests otherwise.

The Secret to Year-On-Year Profits

What I discovered in consistently profitable companies like Southwest Airlines was a very clear mission in service excellence. And service excellence is achieved through *servant leadership*.

Remember that comment from a passenger of Flight 3411 about the airline's supervisor's 'poor leadership?'

Servant leadership, in contrast, is the act of a leader who knows that his role is to serve and ensure the well-being of the people below him. Unfortunately, many of us understand this backward, where we expect the leader to be served instead.

It All Starts at the Top.

In a top private hospital in Singapore from 2000 to 2006, the core tenets of servant leadership were quietly applied, almost as if it was an experiment.

It was a leadership style never before seen in the industry (in Singapore) and it effected a change so positive that the hospital's revenue grew from US$70 million to US$100 million.

I was the CEO of that hospital during those 6 years.

Servant leadership and service excellence were the secret tools that allowed me to motivate employees suffering from depressingly low morale. I also needed to resolve the high staff turnover rate.

When I took office, the hospital was in dire need of motivational and emotional support. The hearts and minds of the staff needed to be taken care of.

But first, I had to 'walk the talk', and exemplify service excellence in my daily actions before I could inspire service excellence in others and empower my employees to care for our customers and patients.

In order to inspire such employees, leaders needed to become the x**servant leader** first—that is the real secret behind some of the world's most successful CEOs.

CHAPTER 2 ▶▶▸

The Alternative: 6-Star Success

The Ritz Experience

On a cold January morning, a guest checked into a multi-week stay at the Ritz-Carlton, Boston Common. He was scheduled to go under the knife at a nearby hospital during this time.

His wife was with him, caring for him and assisting during his sojourn. Although the couple was glad to be with each other, the hotel staff (known internally as the Ladies and Gentlemen of Ritz-Carlton) discerned that the wife was stressed and emotionally drained.

One evening, she found herself at the front desk and requested a second room for the following night from the Front Desk Agent. The 71st *Golden Globe Awards* was airing and the wife was wanting watch the annual ceremony without unsettling her husband's rest.

The perceptive staff at the Ritz were aware of the wife's quiet hardship and the Front Desk Agent led the team to create a personalized experience to help the wife relax and take her mind off her worries.

Together, the Ritz team transformed one of their deluxe rooms into a one-of-a-kind Golden Globes private event.

A fellow Front Desk Agent who worked at the Golden Globes awards ceremony prior to joining the hotel staff threw himself into creating a spectacle that felt as if you were attending the event.

They made a gift bag that was not unlike those handed out to celebrities and VIPs who attended the Golden Globes.

While the gift bag was being put together, the Guest Relations Supervisor chimed in to help decorate the room with flowers, Golden Globe magazines, gold and white balloons and a red carpet made of fresh red rose petals.

As a finishing flourish, the team provided champagne, chocolate-covered strawberries and popcorn for the guests' dining pleasure during the show.

They even sent a special VIP invitation to the guests' room.

When the time came for the broadcast of the Golden Globes, the Front Desk Agent ushered the wife into her room and she was brought to tears at the sight of what had been done for her. With moist eyes, she shared with the Ritz staff how her previous nights had been especially strenuous with her husband's ailing condition and other complications with her loved ones.

She was so grateful to the Front Desk Agent, thanking him several times and expressing her gratitude for going out of his way to create such a magical experience for her.

Even her husband turned up during the broadcast to partake in the festivities and was amazed by the extent that the Ladies and Gentlemen of Ritz-Carlton created a restful and incredibly memorable experience for his wife.

Cross-Industry Expertise

The Ritz-Carlton name goes beyond being a great hotel. Their service standards and excellence have immortalized this organization into a cultural icon, inspiring and appearing often in novels, movies, and even songs.

Authors have referenced the Ritz in stories such as F. Scott Fitzgerald's *The Diamond as Big as the Ritz*, and in E.B. White's novel *The Trumpet of the Swan*. The HBO original series Boardwalk Empire also features the Ritz-Carlton in Atlantic City.

Irving Berlin's song "Puttin' on the Ritz" directly describes living in the hotel, and rapper Plies released the song "Ritz-Carlton" that references spending time enjoying the hotel in no uncertain terms.

If the Ritz could dominate the hospitality industry, popular culture, and maintain high levels of consumer loyalty and advocacy, shouldn't their principles and best practices work well for other businesses as well, hotel or not?

This was the idea that led me to look outside the boundaries of my medical profession to find ways to reinvigorate my employees and create lasting value for my patients.

As the chief executive of my hospital, my instinct told me that we needed to look outside, not in.

We needed to seek practices that have worked for others outside our own industry.

If we continually benchmark ourselves against other companies in the same trade, then we can never add value beyond what we have been doing for the past several years or even decades.

But when we start observing what is working for companies outside our industry and bring those concepts back to our line of work, then new paradigm shifts can occur, creating massive value for both our employees and customers.

Together, my staff and I organized cross-industry training sessions with the Ritz-Carlton, Millenia Singapore.

Here's how we observed and bolstered our hospital practices with hands-on help from the Ritz.

Leadership/Performance Management

In our quest for continued improvements in the hospital, we noted that the service culture in the Ritz is pervasive across all levels of staff. **This was the key and essential as all Ritz employees from the General Manager (GM) to the ground staff embody the hotel's core values.**

At the hospital, not all our senior managers walk-the-talk. We started by having senior managers make routine rounds to the departments and initiating conversations with staff and patients as examples of our service standards. Over time, this encouraged our staff to improve their service delivery to our patients.

Name Tags

Job designations are not displayed on name tags worn by the ladies and gentlemen of Ritz-Carlton. **Their culture revolves around being easily introduced and distinguished by name, and that each staff member is available to serve guests at any given point in time.**

At the hospital, every employee wears name tags that present the wearer's name and designation. We needed to create a culture that does not define an employee by his designation, but to have everyone focused on serving any patient, no matter their role. To foster this culture, we began to remind ourselves to look out for, identify, and render aid to any patients who need help.

Greeting and Escorting Guests

There are no signages or maps in a Ritz-Carlton hotel. **One of their basic protocols is escorting their guests to their requested destination as a personalized service.**

At the hospital, we started a *greet and escort* practice, where employees are encouraged to escort patients to where they want to go. Concierges are also trained to invite patients out of elevators first before walking out themselves.

Daily Line-Ups

Before each shift, the Ritz supervisor will conduct 30-minute briefing sessions where the staff is informed of a recent "Wow" story (like the Golden Globes initiative), complimenting staff to boost morale, highlighting Ritz's 20 Basics of Service as a reinforcement of values, discussing service quality indicators, and updating the team on VIPs and guests with special needs. At the hospital, we do not have briefing sessions for most departments.

We started briefing sessions to keep staff updated on our patients' needs while discussing possibilities for improvement, encouraging each member to share their ideas freely.

Food and Beverage Service

Every member of Ritz-Carlton is knowledgeable about the range of products and services offered by the hotel so that they can best meet the needs of their guests and help other employees.

At the hospital, not all staff members know our products and service etiquette. We have begun training our employees and establishing routine briefing sessions to reinforce their proficiency in our products and service etiquette.
Customer Preference

The Ritz-Carlton staff are trained to recognize the specific needs and requests of guests and record preferences and birthdays in a central database. This system is globally accessible to all Ritz-Carlton hotels and any hotel employee can use the information for a personalized service to guests who revisit the hotel.

At the hospital, our customer service staff has an individual customer preference file. We have put into action the sharing of a Master Customer Preference file to share patient preferences through the computer system so that all employees have accessibility.

Empowerment and Going the Extra Mile

Ritz-Carlton fosters creativity for "Wow" moments by empowering their staff to use up to $2,800 to satisfy the needs of guests. They believe that if it is the right thing for an employee to do, they are allowed to break away from their assigned duties without consulting their supervisors - which motivates their staff to go the extra mile for their guests.

At the hospital, we began inspiring our staff by giving them a $50 fund to present gifts to our patients, such as a basket of fruits, birthday gifts, and even toys for children. Our customer service staff have also started to go the extra mile by helping patients with their shopping, bringing items from their home to their ward, and even facilitating a hair wash for patients who requested for one.

These initiatives were the first steps we took in pursuit of service excellence.

With each passing month, our company-wide effort into customer care at the hospital became a movement within our ranks, growing into a culture that we were proud to call our own. And as we continued our practices, we began listening to our own employees and discovered that quite often, they had ideas that embody the Ritz spirit.

We began introducing free drink vouchers to help calm the nerves of fathers-to-be and offered complimentary limousine services for mothers who had just given birth to their babies. Free massage chairs were provided in our wards, and we distributed handmade, heartfelt flower cards to our VVIP patients.

In 2006, our efforts paid off.

Our hospital was awarded the Asian Hospital Management Award in Best Customer Service. This was based on reception from patients locally and also from around the region (Indonesia, Malaysia, India, and Pakistan).

Our high service ratings also stem from how we care for our foreign patients. We provided a dictionary of top 8 commonly used foreign languages to create first and lasting impressions with foreign patients.

When overseas patients arrive, we realized that they commonly do not travel alone. They usually stayed for three to five days and can bring up to six family members with them. This means that hotel accommodation is required, as well as assistance in local tours, dining locations, and places to shop when they are not visiting the hospital.

This meant that we could not stop at offering only hospital services. We started collaborations with travel agencies to develop exclusive healthcare packages that served the logistical and travel needs of these patients. With our humble roots starting with learning from the Ritz, we created a service-focused culture for ourselves that allowed us to become the service leader in the healthcare industry.

Even Apple Took a Page from the Ritz-Carlton

Steve Jobs asked himself a critical question when Apple was about to launch their very first Apple stores:

"What's the best customer experience you've ever had yourself, as a customer?"

Simple, but profound.

After asking around in his California headquarters, the best customer experience that kept getting brought up was in a

Ritz-Carlton resort. He promptly signed up all his Apple store managers for training at the Ritz-Carlton Leadership Centre.

It was out of this training that gave Apple the idea to start the Genius Bar - which is a cross industry innovation inspired from the concierge desk of the hospitality industry.

As a concierge-style support for Apple customers, employees (also known as Geniuses) are readily available to assist with any problems, be it hardware or software. And why do Apple customers love the Genius Bar?

Because few businesses provide such an amazing experience for their customers - studies have found that 90 per cent of their customers adore the Genius Bar.

It's free, you get attended to by friendly and helpful faces, and you usually walk away "extremely satisfied" or "very satisfied" with the service, according to NPD Group reports (NPD Group, Inc is one of the largest market research companies in the world).

On top of the sky-high customer satisfaction and increasing their sense of affection and loyalty to the brand, someone who visits the Genius Bar is likely to buy another Apple product - talk about win-win!

Apart from the very noticeable concierge-style service that Apple transplanted from Ritz-Carlton, the tech company also incorporated the highly underrated but exceedingly important factor of six-star customer service: the perceptive assistance.

The ladies and gentlemen of the Ritz abide by Gold Standards, one in particular which is, *The Ritz-Carlton experience enlivens the senses, instils well-being, and* ***fulfils even the unexpressed wishes and needs of our guests.***

Similar to the story of the Golden Globes experience, Apple service staff are trained to be attentive and perceptive in picking up on what customers want, but don't express... and that's one of the great secrets behind Apple's ability to build engaged, likely-to-become-loyal customers.

In a world where products and services are becoming increasingly commoditized, service excellence is how your company can truly stand out and become the first choice in a sea of similar competitors who could take over your position in the market.

Perceptive assistance often takes place even *before* the customer has made their way to the Genius Bar. With the touch of a finger, you can schedule an appointment, and the Apple Geniuses will begin preparing for your arrival to immediately assist you *upon* your arrival.

Apple also accomplishes something that few companies even bother to think about - customers do not have to repeatedly introduce their names to each member of the store staff.

Their employees can address their customers by name, even if they were not near enough to hear the customer's name during the first introduction.

The Apple employee that does the initial greeting with the customer quietly shares the name and specifics with the rest of the team so that everyone working at the store is equipped with the customer's name when they step up to provide assistance.

Now, can you say the same is true for Apple's competitors? The goal for Apple is to listen to you, understand what you need, and personalize their service to get you what you're looking for. As you interact with their staff, you feel heard, known, and understood by these cheerful employees and the fruit logo that they represent.

Each member of the Apple customer service team was employed because of their dedication to computers and customer assistance – which is yet another layer of excellence that allowed Apple to amass such a loyal following.

Even when it comes to making payment, which can be unpleasant for customers, Apple takes the edge off by bringing the checkout to you. Your friendly blue-shirted guide will personally present a mobile card reader to you so you can complete the transaction right where you are, instead of queuing at the counter.

Just like how the Ritz takes the utmost care of their guests, so do Apple employees in their perceptive assistance and friendliness.

The Ritz-Carlton's *Gold Standards* (which are proudly displayed on their website) is the culture that every employee embodies, and this culture is that of a service professional.

Just how tech companies, hospitals, and businesses of other industries come to the Ritz to learn how to become service professionals, so can we, no matter how large or small our businesses are.

I'm excited to share with you more about service excellence in the course of this book. My wish for you is to discover that it's not just another business catchphrase, but something that can lead to massive commercial success for your company.

...All in All
(Learning Points)

- When in doubt, learn from those that have been successful before you.
- When it came to learning about top-tier service levels, I couldn't have asked for better than what The Ritz-Carlton provided for my staff.
- Service culture needs to be deeply pervasive for all levels of staff. From the GM to the ground staff, the entire

organization needs to embody the vision, mission, and core values of the organization.

- Creating "Wow" moments are only possible with the help of your staff.
- At the hospital, our customer service staff are empowered with the funding to go the extra mile for our patients.
- Personalized service like greeting by name might sound difficult to include in your service, but a big reason why The Ritz continues its dominance for over three decades is because their staff are trained to recognize the specific needs and requests of guests and record preferences and birthdays.
- To prove that service levels are important in today's business environment (examples from my organizations, The Ritz-Carlton, and Apple notwithstanding), we constantly achieve awards like the Asian
- Hospital Management Award in Best Customer Service. This was based on reception from patients locally and also from around the region (Indonesia, Malaysia, India, and Pakistan).
- Going the extra mile doesn't end at using a corporate fund for patients. We began introducing free drink vouchers to help calm the nerves of fathers-to-be and offered complimentary limousine services for mothers who had just given birth to their babies. What can you do for your company to make customers feel that you care?

CHAPTER 3

"Serving Inside" First

"Code Pink"

It was a Monday evening seemingly like any other when a grey Toyota Corolla headed towards a busy intersection in the city fringe district of Farrer Park, Singapore—with the driver unconscious at the wheel.

The car wasn't going at full speed, but it kept meandering to the right... till the front bumper collided with the guardrail, with two tires riding the curb as the car came to a screeching stop.

The driver had suffered a sudden stroke and was out cold when the Toyota hit the guardrail.

And of all places, he crashed right outside Farrer Park Hospital, an integrated all-in-one healthcare institute with hospital facilities and hotel amenities.

At the time, Nurse Steve Mocsoy had just ended his shift and was heading home when he saw the accident and sprang into action. Farrer Park Hospital has an internal telephone number for responding to medical emergencies in close proximity called

"Code Pink," which Steve promptly activated as he raced to the driver's aid.

When he reached the car, the driver was exhibiting classic signs of a stroke victim, including foaming at the mouth and vomiting.

In less than five minutes, he was joined by six other colleagues with full equipment from the hospital, including two doctors. Moving in a coordinated and highly practised effort, they lowered the seat to a more comfortable position and ensured that the driver's airway was clear so that his breathing would remain uninterrupted.

Together, they stabilized the driver and observed his condition watchfully with an electrocardiogram.

Without the help of this highly responsive team, the driver would have to wait until emergency services arrived, which may have been too late for him. But with the help of the staff from Farrer Park Hospital, he was given the best chance of survival.

The driver was still unconscious when the fire and rescue specialists arrived to extricate him from his car, and remained passed out all the way to the emergency department. The team at Farrer Park Hospital even gave a courtesy call to check on the driver's condition, sending well wishes to him and his family for a speedy recovery.

It might seem like the duty of medical personnel to help someone in an emergency, but not all hospitals have employees who take action to care for others.

There are hospital employees who do not respond to emergencies that are outside their jurisdiction, like in the 2016 case of a lady who was left to die just outside the locked door of the emergency room in a Boston hospital.

The difference is like night and day.

Companies across the world have this problem when their employees only do the minimum required—resulting in minimal success, whether in employee engagement, customer satisfaction, or revenue figures.

Farrer Park's Nurse Mocsoy's quick response to an off-duty accident and Southwest Airlines' care for their passengers far exceeded expectations when it comes to customer service.

But unfortunately, the opposite end of customer service can be observed in cases like the Boston emergency room case and United Airlines' conduct of David Dao's incident.

But how do we propel employees to serve above and beyond—to encourage committed and 'automatic' employee performance that has given rise to massive success for companies, like Southwest Airlines' employees and Apple's Geniuses?

Committed Employees Through Emotional Connection

Companies across the world desire a workforce that's highly engaged and motivated in their jobs. After all, it is in a business' best interests to have higher performing employees who can keep customers satisfied while growing together with the company.

But how do we motivate employees to become committed to their jobs and companies? Is it simply just helping them find joy in their work and giving them desirable salaries and benefits?

If we boil things down to the basic principle, an employee's degree of commitment and engagement is directly related to how they *feel* about the business and the employer.

It is about the emotional connection built as a result of an employee feeling as if they belong to a cause larger than themselves.

Compare this to an employee who is only interested in collecting a paycheck each month. The lengths such an employee would go to for customers and would-be customers would be far less than the actions a committed employee would take. When an employee is committed, they are not fighting for themselves, but as part of a whole that is the company.

The company, in turn, also becomes part of the employee's identity. It's a mutually beneficial relationship.

At the highest level of employee engagement, a fully committed employee would happily tell people that they would work for free – the pay cheque is practically a bonus!

But more importantly, when the workforce is committed and engaged, customers can see it too, which makes them far more likely to interact and purchase your products and services.

Sadly, most companies forget building the all-important emotional connection between them and their employees. Most attempts at building such connections are unspirited and mechanical (what we would often term as "go through the motions") rather than developing real relationships between employees and the company—which is why most employee engagement activities fail to make much difference.

How do we know this is happening?

According to studies conducted by Gallup, two-thirds of employees in their research group were reported to be disengaged and not committed to the companies that they worked for.

What does this mean for your company? Chances are, about 70 per cent or more of your employees are not engaged.

This means that if your employees aren't feeling engaged with your company, even your highest performing talents could walk out of the door at any given point in time.

The lack of real employee engagement is sometimes compounded further by business leaders who demand commitment from their employees, rather than earn it through emotional connections.

Employee Engagement at the Farrer Park Hospital

When we first opened our doors in Farrer Park Hospital in 2016, we were the first fully integrated healthcare-hospitality complex, with an adjoining hotel.

Leading the hospital proved to be a challenge for me (despite 6 years of success managing another hospital in the heart of Singapore), because what worked previously did not work at all for Farrer Park. My initial attempts to engage my staff did not have the same level of positive response that I'd previously experienced, which was a major dilemma. The friendly contests to see who could be the most helpful and welcoming to patients worked wonders to inspire the workforce in my previous hospital, but failed miserably to create a spirited effort in this new hospital.

And then it dawned on me: the employees were not motivated by competition.

My previous employees who enjoyed competition were predominantly local Singaporeans and Malaysians, and we tend to thrive in situations that create winners—activities that encourage scores and "going for gold" was fun for this group of people.

But when I studied my employees at Farrer Park, I realized that most of the people we hired were Filipinos. And it was clear that Filipinos didn't find contests interesting, to say the least. One thing is for sure, though. People from the Philippines are extremely expressive and sociable.

For some reason, all of them sing exceptionally well. As a matter of fact, I've yet to meet one who doesn't sing! Their culture tends to support and praise performances (song, dance, and skit, you name it), and virtually every Filipino owns a karaoke system at home.

So instead of sticking with what worked previously, we decided to adapt to the melodic and theatrical nature of our

The leaders of this company are serious about employee management. So serious that they send their employees on paid vacations—anywhere they wish or prefer.

Their employees are not allowed to do any work, such as answering work-related calls or messages.

Full Contact's philosophy is that employees who go on vacation without being bothered by work will come back fully refreshed and in a better mindset, fully committed to drive the company towards their goals.

On top of these benefits, employees usually return to work with different perspectives, which help them come up with unique solutions to problems.

The hidden benefit of these paid vacations also helps the company erase the assumption that only certain people can solve a problem.

When employees resume work relaxed and find that things have been running smoothly in their absence, they are not stressed about doing everything on their own and can trust their colleagues to perform.

Now that we have talked about 'serving inside', what about 'outside'? We'll talk about that in the next chapter.

...All in All
(Learning Points)

- Developing a culture of employee engagement where the staff are motivated to perform higher and take the initiative to do things above and beyond the realm of their assigned duties starts with *understanding* them.
- When we understand what motivates and encourages them, and we give them that, there is no limit to your company's success because they will fight with you to achieve your goals.

- If we boil things down to the basic principle, an employee's degree of commitment and engagement is directly related to how they *feel* about the business and the employer. It's about the emotional connection built as a result of employees feeling as if they belong to a cause larger than themselves.
- If your employees aren't feeling engaged with your company, even your highest-performing talents could walk out of the door at any given point in time.
- In the next chapter, we'll talk about how we can further support such a culture to maintain and raise the bar for employee engagement and service excellence in your company.

CHAPTER 4 ▶▶▸

Inside-Out Approach

The Process of Employee Engagement

In Chapter Three, we learned that understanding our employees is the driving force behind true employee engagement.

And the secret to understanding them is to think from their point of view and to hear them out.

What stresses them and what keeps them up at night?

What motivates them and engages them to keep fighting for your cause? If you don't know the answers to these questions, there's one incredibly easy way to obtain this golden nugget of information:

Simply ask them.

What are they looking for in your company? A sense of purpose? Financial security? A say in decision-making?

Once you find out what they are looking for, tell them you'll work together as a team to achieve the goal they desire… and be amazed by how hard they are willing to work and how far they're willing to go for you and your company.

That's how you give your staff inspiration that skyrockets motivation levels and dedication to their work.

From off-duty hospital staff who rush to the aid of a patient outside their immediate jurisdiction to cartoon animators who create award winning movies after award-winning movies... It is only possible through an empowered and inspired workforce.

In the large organizations I've led - I held weekly coffee sessions with different groups of staff to get some face-to-face time and to *really* get to know them.

This is not a common practice in many organizations.

Many leaders don't work this so 'close to the ground'. This means that you will not be able to gain the level of insight and an all-rounded perspective vital to a successful leader. But if you don't understand them, how would you serve and lead them?

'Close to the ground' leaders are the only ones who are able to truly understand the men and women in their companies, and their success often goes beyond what is traditionally thought of as achievable.

We call this the "Inside-Out Approach", and it is something that I'm proud to say is instilled in the doctors, nurses, and hospital staff I've led.

A Merry Christmas

Where I live in Singapore, we don't have four seasons because it is summer 365 days a year. It's never a white Christmas in my tropical country, but we do spend it with friends and family.

We exchange presents and enjoy a feast but not everyone gets to do that, especially patients confined to their beds— and the employees of Farrer Park Hospital know that better than most. In their care for the patients under their charge, the employees were painfully aware that most were in no condition to leave the hospital to be with their loved ones.

Some were foreign patients who had planned to travel home for the holidays and barely had anyone in Singapore. But they'd fallen ill and had to be warded for an extended period of time.

Alexandra was one of the patients the doctors and nurses of Farrer Park fondly remember, to this day.

She was terminally ill and in no shape to even get out of bed, let alone travel home.

She and her husband were working as expatriate professionals for a large company in Singapore. But when the illness struck Alexandra, they had no choice but to get her admitted to Farrer Park Hospital and tend to her health till she got better.

Her hospital stay started earlier in the year and extended into Christmas.

She was not alone: hundreds of other patients were in the wards too during this festive season, but the spirit of joy was hard to feel with the pain and discomfort of their ailments weighing them down.

On Christmas Day, many of them were lamenting where they could have been, if they were unburdened by their illnesses or injuries. While still in their thoughts, a group of red-clad elves surprised them by merrily making an entrance to their wards, singing Christmas carols and bringing presents for each and every one of them.

These elves were members of Farrer Park Hospital. By volunteering their time to become an elf on Christmas Day, it meant they were unable to return home to spend the joyous occasion with their respective families.

It was not an easy sacrifice that these Christmas elves had to make, but the result of their actions were the smiles of their patients and the joy in their hearts—many of whom have not felt such mirth since they fell ill.

Some patients were even left absolutely speechless and in tears when they were handed a specially chosen and carefully wrapped present, letting them know that they were far from forgotten during Christmas Day.

That's why each year during this festive season, a 'strike team' of altruistic hospital staff volunteers stay behind to surprise the people under their care and to lighten heavy hearts.

But it takes a special company culture to encourage and empower the staff to care so much for their patients.

It takes an 'Inside-Out' Approach.

Creating Trusting Relationships That Empower Employees

Many employees in Farrer Park Hospital can tell you that one thing they enjoy is the culture of lending a helping hand to one another.

The management also strongly encourages their staff to learn new things, rather than just 'stick with the programme'. To top it off, the salaries are high and the staff are happy with the benefits.

Hospitals in general have a sizable employee base, and it is normal that not every employee will have a corporate email account (about 40 per cent in most large companies). But Farrer Park Hospital did not allow this to get in the way of employee communication.

We leveraged on what we already have—a smartphone in the pocket of almost all members of the hospital. Our staff now use a custom app on their phones that empowers them to be engaged 24/7. On a personal level, the app also helps each employee in the areas of fitness, personalized nutrition, stress management, and social support, in addition to corporate updates.

As hospital professionals, we realized that our nurses are constantly on the go, which is why a smartphone app was the way to engage them with the organization, while encouraging them to stay healthy and learn more.

Newsletters, articles, training calendars, corporate discounts, and many other features are readily available for our staff on the app. But non-smartphone users are not left alone. Notice boards are updated with key messages that keep this group of employees on the same page as the rest of the team.

As the CEO, I needed to interact with these employees and be closer with them, as opposed to a leader who constantly isolates himself within the cold walls of his office.

I began writing weekly motivational messages to the members of the hospital, encouraging them to achieve their goals. I monitor the progress of various teams across the organization to ensure that communication is effective and that the staff members are heard.

To speak to them on a personal level, I found that regular coffee sessions with small groups of employees really helped me to hear them out and listen to any suggestions for improvements that they may have.

Outside their occupations, we also connect with their families through customized programmes such as "Kids @ Work" for the children of employees, and continue engaging with our staff with Corporate Social Responsibility (CSR) activities for employees to contribute back to society.

All employees also undergo training to embrace the "Farrer Service Mindset" to help patients and each other, as well as "The Power of One Team Building" programme that has been measured to increase staff satisfaction, year after year.

It comes as no surprise then, that in December 2016, Farrer Park Hospital took home the award for "Employee Engagement of the Year" under the Health Products and Services industry at the Singapore Business Review Management Excellence Awards event.

Our managers work on the "inside" first and take care of our own, so that our employees feel engaged, that their voice matters, and they are free to produce the best work they are capable of delivering.

Inside-Out Approach in Other World-Class Companies

In a study of over one million employees, *Harvard Business Review* reports that workers are the most likely to switch jobs at the one-year mark.

While most companies see this as a normal turnover trend, one Los Angeles mobile gaming studio refuses to think the same way.

As a renowned and acclaimed company in the industry that has produced no less than six games that have reached number one in app download charts, Scopely knows a thing or two about retaining employees and creating a favourable and enjoyable environment for them. After all, how can you produce fun, best-selling games without having employees that have fun in the process of making them?

Scopely engages its employees around yearly milestones, often with amusing and sometimes downright bizzare gifts.

One employee received a custom-made samurai sword, while others got exclusive oil paintings of themselves in the act of comical relief. One such oil painting featured the employee posing with a Viking helmet, one hand on a ukulele and another grasping a bottle of beer.

Their approach to engaging their employees has been the cornerstone to keeping their best staff, while allowing them to perform at the highest level to consistently produce the best games in the world, again and again.

It can be summed up in one word: fun.

This, unfortunately, is lacking in far too many companies, often because leaders think that 'fun' is the opposite of productivity and they are afraid of challenging themselves to move outside the box and their comfort zone.

But that's the furthest from the truth. By providing this one authentic element of fun, companies like Scopely have proven that the reverse is actually true.

Motivation increases, things get done more effectively and creatively, and everyone is generally happier!

One brand that needs no introduction is Netflix.

In the past ten years, their innovation has caused a dramatic shift in the way we consume movies and TV programmes. And when Patty McCord took the helm as the company's first Chief Talent Officer, she wanted to revamp the way they did things for the better.

Many companies believe that there will only be a small group of 'best performing' employees - which means that the rest are either 'average' or will have to be replaced.

This assumption for hiring 'talent', however, is incorrect—it overlooks the training, development, and proper employee placement that eventually enables people to become expert performers.

But why replace when you can simply hire 'best performers'?

The challenge McCord had was to sort the "best performers" from the rest, but her team rose to the challenge in a way that runs counter to the hiring policies of most companies. She focuses on character rather than skills or experience. They were highly meticulous in hiring only mature, understanding team players who can think of the needs of others rather than just their own.

The result?

Netflix won the most Emmy nominations in a year, beating HBO's seemingly infallible reign after 17 years.

McCord discovered that instead of working harder to inspire staff who may or may not be high-performing team players, why not hire them right from the get-go. She believed in bringing in people with both talent and character, so they can work well within the company and come up with what the rest of the world considers as unbelievable results.

It is an undeniable fact that this style of 'Inside-Out' hiring policy has led to the massive billion-dollar success of Netflix and their stellar employee retention rate.

Emergent Leadership

Empowering employees to perform independently and demonstrate their own leadership initiative has been another core component of my management role in various organizations.

Of the different reasons why our revenue kept growing year-on-year, I attribute the success mostly to the environment that I built, allowing each person the space to act 'without authority'. This meant that they are allowed to make many decisions on their own without the need to ask for approval from a superior.

An example of how we created this environment is the GST (Greet, Smile, and Thank) platform that my management team and I set-up, which encouraged strong team cohesion and passionate purpose in their work.

The 'greet and escort practice' that we talked about in Chapter Two was an extension of the GST platform, ultimately realizing each employee's full potential, especially in their creative and innovative abilities.

With the help of the men and women in the organizations I've led, we achieved feats that would not have been possible without the "emergent environment" that inspired the productive and creative solutions that we became known for.

In the early 2000s, we launched bold, never-before-seen customer engagement projects in the healthcare industry that eventually became more of a norm in the present day.

Our teamwork resulted in a McDonald's playground in the children's ward, a spa in the maternity ward, installation of OSIM massage chairs for anxious fathers awaiting the birth of their newborns, handwritten encouragement notes by nurses at the neonatal intensive care unit, and even presenting patients with personalized greetings.

To be honest, I didn't expect the effects of our work to have such massive positivity with patients and staff alike. But the numbers don't lie. One key indicator that we were on the right track were our 8-figure annual growth reports.

The secret behind our success is a surprisingly simple one.

We, as an organization, always act with our patients' interests first.

In order to facilitate this, my management team and I always act in our employees' best interest first. In the next chapter, we'll dive into more examples and case-studies of such results that "serving inside" and approaching "inside-out" can produce, like American multinational automaker Ford's 200,000 employee example.

All in All

(Learning Points)

- Sometimes, we forget that the best way for leaders to lead employees is not from a top-down, 'command and control' authoritative approach.
- Instead, we work for them. We work to provide an income, stability, and a safe environment so that they can perform and grow. And when employees are allowed to perform and grow, the company grows as well.

- Most importantly, we need to find out what drives or motivates them and what their perspectives are through talking to them. You will receive invaluable insight and perhaps even advice which you may otherwise never be able to obtain.
- Listening to them is how we can encourage committed and 'automatic' employee performance that has given rise to massive success for companies, like Southwest Airlines' employees and Apple's Geniuses.
- The most successful way I've found to listen to them is to have weekly face-to-face coffee sessions with different groups of employees.
- Finally, we need to provide and encourage an organizational mindset of growth. This allows employees to feel that they have the "elbow room" to take risks, innovate, and even go beyond their mandate if needed, without fear of undue punishment.

CHAPTER 5

Serving from the Heart

Achieving Six-Star Service Standards

Looking at the examples in the past few chapters, it is evident that achieving six-star service comes first from having a six-star employee experience.

After all, how can you expect an excellent level of service from your employees if you aren't providing them with a satisfactory work experience?

As our world evolves more into the digital setting with ever-increasing Internet speed and 24/7 connectivity, it is inevitable that the workforce today expects an enriching, productive, and enjoyable time at work. Millennials today have been extremely vocal about management and Human Resource (HR) practices, raising the bar when it comes to employee feedback and satisfaction.

However, few companies are able to achieve the level of employee engagement that Dreamworks or Netflix have managed to attain.

A study by Glassdoor (an online platform where current and former employees anonymously review companies) that measured employee engagement across thousands of businesses in 2016 and 2017 showed us that engagement levels did not change much between the years.

These engagement levels have been measured to remain at the same level over the period of two years:

Balancing personal and work obligations (Providing a healthy work-life balance, where the needs of personal and professional responsibilities are equally taken care of.)

Aligning employees' ideals with the company's vision (Educating employees about the purpose of the organization, and creating an environment where employees can feel meaningful and purpose in their work.

Empowering employees with programmes specific to age brackets (Equipping employees with various programmes for younger, older, or multi-generational personnel that will support all segments of the entire workforce.)

Using design philosophy to develop the employees' journey (Design philosophy is all about the user experience—in this case, it is about designing a journey that encourages your employees to thrive and perform.)

The challenge stems from a rather tight perspective on 'best practices' for employee engagement that may or may not apply to different organizations.

Instead of focusing so narrowly on engagement, the management's perspective has to shift towards a more encompassing view of the entire employee journey, and fully leveraging on tools to facilitate feedback, interaction, and employee self-service (like in the Farrer Park Hospital mobile app).

The management teams are also not prioritizing employee experience— most companies only perform a survey once a year as their employee engagement exercise. In fact, some companies have not appointed a senior executive or team to build and enrich the employee experience.

As with most companies, isolated departments often find it hard to obtain resources for programmes that may not have been budgeted for.

This is especially true for an HR department when it comes to planning for workplace benefits and tools that help create a positive employee experience.

The Need For Feedback

Employee feedback is often seen as an optional thing for most businesses but in many high-performing companies, it is mandatory.

For me, it is no different. In the two hospitals that I have served as CEO, I've always had weekly coffee sessions with my employees scheduled religiously. There is a time and place for online feedback forms, but there's no replacement for talking directly to a member of your organization.

The insight I gained from these face-to-face talks were highly valuable and I could help to motivate them by offering them a listening ear and taking their suggestions seriously. Other than hearing their feedback and recommendations, I also take the time to explain our company's vision and core principles that help to guide their day-to-day work.

I also believe in a 100 per cent open-door policy. Everyone in my organization is entitled to walk through my door and have a sit-down session with me. If you catch me in the corridors, I'm always prepared to chat with you!

It is my belief that such candidness and openness give employees a more personal connection to me and the organization–a connection that serves as the foundation of employee engagement.

After all, I serve them, not the other way around.

With this belief, my team has managed to prove the workability and practicality of our approach, where we build leaders at all levels of the organization.

In 2016, we gained recognition for our novel approach, when Farrer Park Hospital won the Best New Hospital of the Year in Asia Pacific from Global Health and Travel Magazine, as well as the Asian Hospital Management Award from Hospital Management Asia (Asia's Leading Conference for Managing Hospitals).

Our other accolades in 2016 also include the Enterprise Innovation Award from Questex and the Management Excellence Award by the Singapore Business Review (SBR).

At SBR's Management Excellence Awards Ceremony, we took home the Employee Engagement of the Year award.

Farrer Park Hospital was selected by SBR's panel of esteemed judges who qualified our winning formula of empowerment, innovation, and technology that we combined with traditional staff engagement methods.

The selection criteria were based on the effectiveness of the strategies that we implemented and its impact to the workforce, including engaging employees and enhancing their level of fulfilment in their careers.

In 2017, we continued our upward progress as an awardee of the Human Resources Magazine (HRM) Awards, known as the Oscars of HR. At the HRM Awards 2017, Farrer Park Hospital clinched the Special Recognition for Best HR Transformation through Technology.

This award acknowledges Farrer Park Hospital's transformation of our HR processes through the use of technology to increase efficiency, allowing us to keep up with the rapidly changing global environment.

Specifically, we were recognized for our efforts to launch the Farrer Park Staff App for our staff to access a range of services (which includes newsletters/articles, training calendar, corporate discounts, health and wellness programmes, push notification and more).

We also clinched the Best Recruitment Evaluation Technique from the Asia Recruitment Awards by the Human Resources Magazine.

To set ourselves ahead of the competition, we worked hard to attain the identity of the most awarded private hospital in Singapore. And through our efforts, I am proud to say that in 25 months, my wonderful, diligent and hard working team managed to earn 25 awards!

If this doesn't prove that our mindset and strategies to engage our staff and listen to employee feedback are effective (not just for ourselves but for your organization too), then I don't know what will!

The lack of employee feedback in many organizations is directly related to why companies are facing many problems such as low staff morale and unsatisfactory performances. In a study published by Deloitte in 2017 on hundreds of companies, only 23 per cent believed that their workforce is aligned with their vision.

84 per cent of the companies surveyed claim to have practices in place that assess work-life balance, but only 23 per cent believe that their practices are effective.

On a global scale, companies that top the charts tend to come from Nordic countries, the Americas, and Europe. Companies in Asia, Africa, and the Middle East rank much lower.

Just as Southwest Airlines went against the grain and put their employees first, so must we realize why they did so, and embrace this principle ourselves.

If you prioritize employees, they will be able to take care of your customers, which will take care of your shareholders.

The vast majority of companies, however, operate in the *opposite* way. There is a pressure to give shareholders priority, which reverses the entire process.

This often leads to short-term gains that seem acceptable on paper but can have highly detrimental long-term effects that culminate in employee dissatisfaction and high turnover rates. Companies are often caught unaware when the early results fade away, which leaves them confused and unable to continue the initial success.

High-performing companies, on the other hand, have found ways to infuse positivity and fulfilment into the employee experience. This creates an environment for purposeful and productive work that enables sustainable, long-term success.

Ford's 200,000 Employee Example

We remember Ford Motor Co. as the company that revolutionized the automotive industry by developing the world's first car moving assembly line in 1913.

They are the legendary manufacturers who produced the iconic Mustang (remember *Gone in Sixty Seconds* starring Nicholas Cage?). The Ford Mustang continues to remain as the symbol of American muscle cars and is a customer favourite till today.

But even Ford, with offices in over 40 countries and more than 200,000 employees, realized the need to reinvent and reinvigorate themselves.

After over a hundred years of success, they are shifting gears to adapt in a new industry climate where clean energy is becoming the next big thing, among other innovations like electrification, self-driving cars, and mobile apps that help drivers find parking spaces and co-share their cars.

It doesn't mean they have to reinvent the wheel, but if the company aims to stay relevant today and achieve a breakthrough in the industry, they will need to start with the people working day-to-day in their offices and factories.

In order to support their business processes, Ford is placing a massive focus on its HR team, with emphasis on workforce solutions and programmes that enhance the lives of their employees.

Their Group Vice President of HR and Corporate Services believes that their "mission is to make employees' lives better by changing the way we think about work, feel about work, and the way we do our work differently."

Ford sought to improve the employee experience by starting with a three-week worldwide strategy lab which involved HR leaders from around the world and the executive team. It was from this initiative that helped Ford come up with an integrated employee engagement plan and a clear HR vision.

And it didn't just come from the top: The Ford HR team rolled out an in-depth survey that allowed their staff to voice opinions, talk about their individual experiences, and appraised which HR programmes were working or not working—across the entire company. Every area of Ford's business was involved.

It was the first time since 1903 that the company had executed such an all-encompassing feedback initiative. From this extensive and earnest drive to accrue employee opinion, the HR team is able to obtain critical information on what their workforce truly wants, their problems, and how they can help and empower their employees in their work.

To facilitate this new drive towards productive employee engagement, Ford divided their staff into three groups: employees, people leaders, and union council leaders.

Ford went a few steps further, establishing more than 30 employee focused "moments that matter" for each of these three groups. Examples of these "moments" ranged from personal statements that empowered an employee to perform in a new position, to helping a Ford staff member understand their place in the company and letting them feel that their opinions are heard and valued by the management.

Does this make you think of Ritz-Carlton's practice of 'Wow' moments for their employees in Chapter Two? If so, you are on the right track! In the hospitals I've led, our executive team ensures that this action is practised daily.

Ford remains committed and focused on their four-year HR campaign, which is highly aligned with the company's vision to improve their business processes.

It is a simple lesson for business leaders: if you focus on your employees, your HR team can significantly enhance the employee experience and empower your staff to become much more productive and effective in their work.

As Ford accelerates into their employee empowerment campaign, we can expect their customers to benefit and engage more with the business, which will raise the bottom line. When the above has happened, their shareholders will be rewarded by the long-term gains achieved by the company.

Embracing Employee Experience

It's not just Ford. Across the globe, more and more companies are discovering the need for employee experience—or risk l osing out to a competitor while your workforce remains disengaged.

If the competition has implemented programmes that improve their employee experience, you can expect their staff to be highly productive and purposeful, with a clear sense of direction.

We see this in companies that are known for their innovation. They look inwards, to their employees for the inspiration to drive themselves forward.

"Hackathons", a "sprint-like" event that usually involves software companies to quickly accomplish an objective by "hacking it out", has been used by companies like Cisco, Pandora, Adobe, and Airbnb to collect employee ideas and to spark new methods that help to engage and keep employees productive and satisfied.

On the executive team, Airbnb has a Chief Employee Experience Officer who is designated to serve employees in effective and creative ways. Some examples are a healthy food programme that their employees are happy with, and equipping their teams with the latest technology. Their workspaces are designed and highly optimized for a highly productive and enriching work environment.

Cisco and Pandora also embrace the need for an engaged workforce with an appointed Chief Employee Experience Officer.

Adobe goes somewhat further by reorganizing its customer experience organization with its HR business units to create a "Customer and Employee Experience" organization. This signifies Adobe's focus and acknowledgment on the people who are the main drivers of their business: employees and customers.

Their HR mission is aimed at allowing employees to feel that their needs and time are respected, and the company is committed to building a long-term relationship with them. Adobe seeks to engage every single one of their employees, no matter their position in the company.

High-performing companies study their employees and the workplace to create an environment that maximizes satisfaction and productivity for their people.

We've observed this effect in Facebook's new 2018 Gehry-designed campus with a redwood forest and rooftop garden that's beautifully constructed, and is brimming with food, collaboration, and exercise spaces.

Happy Employees Make Happy Customers

The takeaway here is a straightforward one:

If you make your employees happy, your customers and shareholders, in turn, will be happy, but this process cannot occur in the opposite sequence.

It has to start with your workforce.

It is about creating an environment where your employees can thrive. A place where they feel satisfied, respected, and empowered to perform at the best of their ability.

Do they feel taken care of? Do they feel that they've been heard? When was the last time you've received and taken action on employee feedback?

If you are having a hard time answering these questions, perhaps it's time to gather the people leaders in your company to address the need for employee experience.

But most importantly... *listen* to your employees.

If global enterprises like Ford, Airbnb, and Facebook are placing such a huge importance on the employee experience, and are multi-million dollar successes themselves, it's safe to say that this focus on employees is a critical element not just to them, but to your company's success too.

In the following chapters, we will be discussing specific action points that you can put into practice almost immediately and see the results of a truly engaged and productive employee base.

All in All
(Learning Points)

- As leaders, we cannot expect excellent levels of service from employees if we aren't providing them an engaging and enriching work experience.
- Instead of focusing so narrowly on engagement, the management's perspective has to shift towards a more encompassing view of the entire employee journey and fully utilizing tools to facilitate feedback, interaction, and employee "self-service" through the growth mindset in setting up the organization and its work groups.
- Employee feedback is critical to discover employees' valuable feedback and recommendations, as well as motivating and encouraging them in their work.
- High-performing companies, on the other hand, have found ways to infuse positivity and fulfilment into the employee experience. This creates an environment for purposeful and productive work that enables sustainable, long-term success.
- Placing a focus on employee experience can result in a highly productive and purposeful workforce, striving forward in unison with a clear sense of direction.

CHAPTER 6

How To Put Excellence Into Service

Turning Play Into Productivity

In hospitals (and in most businesses), most leaders in such organizations are familiar with the benefits of excellent service, yet few think of it as a requirement in the work that they do.

Even fewer place it as a top priority - which is why most customers don't feel like they are being served by staff who really care about their experience of the product or service.

It is why customers don't stay loyal to most brands. They switch companies in a heartbeat.

But when customers finally discover a company that goes above and beyond, it forges within them a deep sense of loyalty and commitment to the brand. Think Disneyland. Or Apple. Or Amazon.

In most theme parks, you simply hop on a few rides and head home afterwards. But when you're in Disneyland, you never want to leave! Their employees consistently exude this enthusiastic, hospitable disposition, creating a welcoming environment that makes Disneyland the "happiest place on Earth".

They are absolutely delighted *just* to have you there.

At Apple, you have extremely passionate service staff who are more than happy to answer your queries and sort out any issues you may have with your MacBook or iPhone.

And as the world's largest online retailer, Amazon's sky-high customer service rankings are attributed to their core commitment to the consumer, with employees who are highly trained in the art of *listening*, and not just having "cut-and-dry" conversations with the customer.

The billion-dollar successes of these companies are predicated on a simple idea:

Service, when done right, results in immense customer satisfaction and massive commercial success.

However, most companies work backwards—they focus on commercial success and leave service excellence on their "(never)-to-do list" – which results in failure or at best, mediocre results.

So how do we put excellence into our service like these giants did?

I use a framework called the FISH! Philosophy (Christensen, 1998).

In my first tenure as CEO, this framework allowed me to revitalize and energize a hospital from the verge of becoming just another commoditized medical organization to becoming an award-winning organization that earned several local and regional accolades.

Following that, I used the same core framework to help Farrer Park Hospital, the second organization that I served as the Chief Executive.

Here, we earned the unprecedented achievement of one award per month during my time leading the company as CEO: 25 awards in 25 months!

The FISH! Philosophy is inspired and modeled after the Pike Place Fish Market in Seattle, and written in the book *Fish! A Remarkable Way to Boost Morale and Improve Results* by Stephen C. Lundin, Harry Paul, and John Christensen.

The philosophy consists of 4 simple parts:

1. Play
2. Choose Your Attitude
3. Make Your Customers' Day
4. Be There

1. Play

At the Pike Place Fish Market in Seattle, USA (which I personally visited), the first thing you'll notice are the boisterous and highly energetic fishmongers, shouting, singing, and throwing their fish and seafood to each other, and even to their customers!

If you are lucky, you can catch them chasing after squealing customers while brandishing a whole octopus, threatening to touch them with a tentacle - all in the name of fun.

When I saw the results of such a fun-spirited and enjoyable environment, I committed myself to applying the same idea at the first hospital I served as CEO.

In our Neonatology department, we care for mothers and newborn infants who need intensive care. I couldn't literally start throwing defibrillators and syringes around in my hospital the way the locals from the Pike Place Fish Market did, but I could apply a similar principle.

While most healthcare facilities exhibit dull facades that couldn't be more depressing to a patient, we started decorating the ceilings and walls of neonatal Intensive Care Units with festive ornaments and created a playful and cheery atmosphere, which was something that the patients undergoing critical medical attention sorely needed.

Soon after we began this new initiative, my staff began to behave more like the fishmongers from Pike Place: they were having fun with a purpose, enjoying the act of decorating for the benefit of their patients.

The staff were no longer simply 'going through the motions' but started to genuinely care for the patients under their care. They sincerely asked the patients how they were doing, and eventually delivered the 6-star service that we ultimately became renowned for.

The patients, too, experienced a service that was a rarity in healthcare. The effect was phenomenal - a tremendous decrease in our surveys on stress and discomfort, and improvements in recovery rates.

'Play' is such a fundamental part of being human, but few businesses ever consider this to be a vital part of running a successful organization.

As a company, recognizing and implementing this core human trait will reap astounding results, especially if you are running a business-to-consumer (B2C) business.

Just like how the Pike Place fishmongers play with their customers and how Disneyland employees offer warm, welcoming smiles to each and every guest, think of how you can meaningfully introduce 'play at work'— it will offer your employees a sense of purpose and belonging that could give you immeasurable results.

2. Choose Your Attitude

'Play at work' is more of a macro initiative that affects the company as a whole, but creating a holistic environment involves going down to the individual level.

Each and every staff needs to be empowered to make the decision to:

➢ **Serve Unconditionally**

If an employee serves with a self-seeking agenda in mind, customers are able to instinctively detect it.

For instance, a sales associate may have his mind set primarily on earning commissions, instead of serving his customers. When this happens, customers know that their best interests are not taken care of, and are prone to turn to an alternative solution... which will be the closest competitor.

Ironically, if he were to do the opposite and put his customers first, his earnings would skyrocket more than he could believe.

But the issue does not simply end with the loss of one or two customers.

Looking at this from a bigger picture, this sales associate represents what your company values to your customers.

Now, those customers that your sales associate comes in contact with may get the impression that your company is only driven by monetary gains and does not care about their customers' needs.

They may even spread the news to their network of friends and acquaintances, and it only takes a few individuals to besmirch your reputation, resulting in unfavourable reviews, fewer customers, and poor sales—creating a vicious cycle.

That is why employees across the organizational hierarchy need to be trained and reminded to put the client before themselves. When they start to serve beyond monetary gains, the reverse is true: clients can detect genuine care and selfless concern, which leads to long lasting relationships that bolster strong, recurring sales.

A servant-leader understands that service and value should be given first without any notion of receiving, after which sales and business success will naturally come.

➢ Endure Difficulty to Deliver Results

We live in an era where it takes seconds to find an answer on Google and only takes a couple of finger-taps to hire an Uber to get you to anywhere you want to be.

Likewise, we often maintain the misconception that results should come instantaneously. But more often than not, they don't! A leader needs to educate staff to persist in the face of difficulty and practise patience and resoluteness.

After all, Rome wasn't built in a day—they continued to lay bricks and pave the roads hour to hour. Moreover, if your company has been plagued by a toxic culture for some time, it is definitely not going to be resolved in one day. Depending on the severity, it may require years.

Train and encourage your staff to understand that results take time, and every minute spent on working towards the goal is another minute towards success.

➢ Remember Customers' Preferences

When it comes to making customers happy, one of the sure-fire certain ways to put a big smile on their faces is to show them that you remembered their preferences.

As a leader, we might not be privy to such information, but you can begin such a culture by asking your employees what they remember about each client, and empower them to actively meet the customers' preferences they remember.

With today's technology and establishing a simple workplace process, we are able to record relevant preferences in Customer Relationship Management systems in the hospitals I've served in. It's a quick and permanent solution to capture customers' preferences before they slip from memory.

This is one of the smallest things that have yielded huge, long-term paybacks in the organizations that I've proudly been a part of.

Here's another example: A father-to-be waits nervously for his pregnant wife to deliver his first-born child. In the waiting room, a nurse smiles and hands him a warm cup of tea, because this attentive nurse had remembered that he wasn't a coffee drinker, and preferred Earl Grey instead.

It would undoubtedly be a pleasant surprise for the father-to-be, who will certainly remember this small act of thoughtful kindness.

Because of this single act (which would later also be supported by similar actions from other employees), he's likely to choose that particular hospital for all future medical needs his family may require.

The takeaway is clear: small gestures of thoughtfulness that emphasize genuine concern over the well-being of your customers will establish the foundation of a loyal, satisfied relationship with your customers in many years to come.

➢ Value the Joy of Serving and Giving

It might take some time to get past the initial inertia of developing a serving and giving culture in your company, but once it takes root, it will become second nature.

When this happens, the staff will begin to act in an authentic and committed manner, not just because it is their job, but because it brings them personal joy to serve.

You can experience this phenomenon in Disneyland. Every staff member is simply happy to be in Disneyland, happy that *you are* in Disneyland, and happy to serve *you*.

That in turn, makes *you* as the guest, happy to be there. You'd never want to leave!

Now, imagine if you could replicate this phenomenon in your business, where your customers never want to leave you. You are proud of the value you're providing, your customers are satisfied with the experience you're offering them, and this mutual positivity becomes the bedrock of business longevity.

➢ (be) Attentive to the Needs of the Customer

When your internal culture is customer-centric and your staff are empowered to serve, the experience that your company presents its customers could become a thing of legend.

This happened consistently in the hospitals that I served as CEO.

A member of my hospital staff, Mr. Mohamed, was a valet who escorted patients from the car to the lobby. He noticed that during rainy days, patients are sometimes unable to avoid getting drenched by the rain. He suggested that we invest in some 'super-large' umbrellas with our logo to keep our patients dry.

This simple, low-cost, yet highly effective idea became a unique service that resulted in leaving our patients with an extremely favourable impression.

Other examples of customer-oriented projects include free limousines for mothers with newborn infants, complimentary drinks for fathers-tobe, free massage chairs in patient waiting rooms and labour wards, highly customized and hand-made flower memos for customers in the 'VVIP' category, and verbal greetings in different languages to form an impression for foreign customers.

When your company embraces such a culture, word gets around about your legendary service, which results in more customers and increasing sales... without spending a dime on advertising!

➢ Never Run Dry

Your sales staff should never feel like they are taking from themselves when they are serving and giving. If the behaviour is adequately inculcated, then it should be a naturally fulfilling experience for the staff themselves.

However, employees getting burnt out is a possible risk that must be managed.

In the hospitals I led, we implemented quarterly lifestyle talks for staff and offered rewards based on the behaviour that represents the culture that we wanted to build.

The talks served as a discussion point to let our staff know that we are listening and watching out for them, and also assisted as a two-way conduit for staff to express their pains and frustrations, so that we could resolve any challenges and reinforce the positivity we needed.

In Farrer Park Hospital, I took this further by arranging 'Coffee Sessions With The CEO' so I could meet employees in groups and personally hear exactly what they needed from them.

The rewards served as additional incentives to motivate employees to joyfully serve and give in their day-to-day work.

These two elements act as the twin anchors that allowed our employees to continue their industry-leading performance as top-of-the-line service staff.

➢ Treat Customers Like Loved Ones

For your employees to fully develop the "service excellence" mindset, they must care for the customer as if they were part of their own family.

That means that the customers' pains are their pains to relieve, the customers' fears are their fears to soothe, and the customers' frustrations are their frustrations to pacify.

Just one would go above and beyond to care for their own family, a customer-centric employee should treat each and every customer as if they were their very own brother or sister.

An effective leader will do well to kickstart such a culture by setting the best example. By genuinely treating employees as if they were valued family members, employees will eventually take notice.

It may not come naturally to everyone, so regularly scheduled reminders to help employees remember will go a long way to inspire and perpetuate the culture of treating customers like they are loved ones.

This is how *natural customer* service is developed in an organization.

You might have realized that these pointers spell out S.E.R.V.A.N.T. and that's how the mindset of a leader should be.

It's a simple acronym to help us remember the core tenets of leadership and a reminder of our duty to serve.

3. Make Your Customers' Day

After you have successfully inculcated a sense of positivity amongst your employees, your next step is to actively 'transfer' this attitude actively to customers every day. In short, it's time to put things into motion and create a cycle of perpetual positivity!

Most companies make it their mission to keep their customers satisfied, but that does not make their experience amazing enough that they want to share it with their network of friends.

To achieve word-of-mouth accolades from your customer, you need to offer an experience that goes above and beyond what is expected.

By under-promising, and over-delivering, you can create a 6-star service that amazes everyone who comes into contact with your brand. Let's see how Apple did it with their iPhone launch.

During the age of inexpensive mobile phones designed to only meet the minimum expectations of customers, Apple redefined the entire industry because they paid close attention to customers' needs, and far exceeded their expectations.

In stark contrast to analog cell phones, the iPhone used a multi-touch touchscreen that allowed users to navigate with relative ease, while seamlessly integrating the traditional numeric keypad and keyboard, which gave rise to a whole new industry in the form of mobile applications.

This revolutionary reinvention of the cell phone was purely focused on the customer's experience, and today, the multi-touch touchscreen has become a necessary feature included by all major cell phone manufacturers.

In fact, Steve Jobs was so devoted to customer experience that 6 weeks before the release of the first iPhone, Jobs replaced the plastic screen with a glass screen because the screen of the prototype he carried in his pocket had been scratched by his keys.

He didn't want customers to be negatively affected by this possibility that he experienced himself, and resolved it even in the face of impossibly tight deadlines and lower profit margins.

As a product-based company, it is important to deliver a product that far exceeds the expectations of your customer, especially when it's a product that the customer uses every day. That's how you truly make their day, to the point where they want to show off or display your product to each and every one of their friends.

In the service industry, the same principle applies.

Employees who face customers frequently on the job like sales associates, cashiers, and customer service representatives need to be highly trained in the practice of listening to customers.

That's how they can provide an experience on a personal level that differentiates you from the rest of the industry.

4. Be There

The primary factor that separates ordinary customer service and an extraordinary experience with your company is whether your staff are *really* there.

That's because most of us are there physically, but are neither mentally nor emotionally present.

For digital companies (especially Software-as-a-Service businesses), it's far too easy to take a step back and let your website do all the work. But when it comes to problems, most companies that promise 24/7 support often end up doing not much more than putting customers on hold.

This rarely happens with Amazon.

They strengthened customer support with a highly accessible Frequently-Asked-Questions section, and offer community-based forums, where fellow customers can rely on the public's collective wisdom to receive help.

If these two options don't work out, help through a personal interaction is an easy option with 24/7 customer service officers ever-ready and always on standby. Amazon is a rare 'web-based' company that has long had a customer service helpline that you can actually call into to get help with the website, billing, or other technical problems.

Amazon even exceeds expectations with some of their products featuring a "Mayday" button that grants users immediate video access to a member of the technical team. It's a strong example of how being actively involved in your business processes and personal contact with customers goes a long way in establishing long-term success.

When it comes to checking on your staff and finding out if they are fully present during their personal, face-to-face interactions with customers, you can simply ask them a simple question of how their day went, then ask them to discuss the details.

If they struggle to provide the details, or aren't able to hold a solid conversation for more than a few minutes, it is likely that your staff are not being mentally present in their work. They may be thinking about their laundry that needs to be done, or how badly a team meeting went, or they may simply be mulling over a personal issue.

Being fully present actually takes practice.

That's when mental training and regular reminders can really help your staff reset psychologically and steer themselves to focus on the task at hand.

Remember - it's not about 'calling out' or shaming your staff who are not mentally present. It's about investing in training, and checking in to grow the capabilities of your employees.

And if you think investing in your employees to create new levels of service excellence is going to be costly, then the next chapter may change your mind.

In the next chapter, you may be surprised at the resourcefulness of your employees, even with low to zero monetary cost.

All in All
(Learning Points)

- ✦ Start with the human need to play, and infuse it into your everyday operations at work—it's the sure-fire way to lift employee morale and skyrocket customer satisfaction!
- ✦ Since doing this is rare in most companies, injecting the concepts explained in this chapter into your business will immediately set you apart from your competition and create a new position for yourself in your industry.

- On an individual level, each employee needs to choose to be positive in their work, and it's done through being a happy **S.E.R.V.A.N.T.** and remembering the meaning behind the acronyms:
  - Serve Unconditionally
  - Endure Difficulty to Deliver Results
  - Remember Customers' Preferences
  - Value the Joy of Serving and Giving
  - Attentive to Customers' Needs
  - Never Run Dry
  - Treat Customers like Loved Ones
- In customer interactions, it is all about channeling your internal positivity outwards to the customer to make their day through:
- A brilliant product that exceeds expectations like Apple's iPhone, or
- Listening to customers in service-based industries and taking care of them.
- The final step in the FISH! Philosophy is to guide your staff away from zoning out or "going through the motions", and train them to become mindful of the present, especially with customers.
  - This is a core tenet of customer service, which is a trait that has allowed Amazon to become a trillion-dollar success.
  - It's not about 'calling out' your staff who are not mentally present. It's about investing in regular training, reminders, and checking in to get them trained in being in the present.
- If a fish market with no formal training can do it, so can you!

CHAPTER 7

It Doesn't Mean You Need a Big Budget...

It's the Little Things That Count the Most

FedEx once had to make delivery using a helicopter. To many, the package delivered was not worth the stress – but the brand did it to keep its promise to a client.

This story has often been told and retold in brand identity discussions, and it goes a long way to show the extent some brands will go when they put the customer first.

Ensuring the satisfaction of your customer is not just a good way to promote your brand, but to also build customer loyalty and business longevity.

And customer satisfaction is not a concept that should apply to only one department, but across the entirety of your organization.

Achieving optimal customer satisfaction demands that the company builds a mindset towards it. And it's important to note that it's not only the thought that matters, but also a genuine concern for customers that leads to the most relevant action steps. It has to reflect genuinely in all the brand identity elements of the company, from the behaviour of the staff members to senior managers.

You'll see it in the little things.

In verbal greetings to an in-store customer. In written replies to an email enquiry. In digital media to an online audience.

And when things go wrong, that's where organizations with customer satisfaction as a core value really shine... compared to companies that only put a priority on cash flow.

Many companies think that they need to spend large sums of money to gain customer satisfaction. They think about setting aside a large sum of money to buy gifts for their customers, or throw in extra goodies to a company purchases – ideas which require a budget which may or may not be approved in the end.

When companies think this way, it often leads to "analysis paralysis" that causes inaction.

Without any action – there won't be any increase in customer satisfaction!

Spending money is not always the answer to reach a goal.

For instance, when the Head of Customer Service of my hospital took charge of the department, she was faced with a task others would have called impossible. She was assigned to improve customer engagement – on a strict $500 budget (In 2019, that would be the equivalent of about $365 USD).

To everyone's amazement, our patients had nothing but the best to say about our service, and our customer satisfaction could not be higher!

How did she and her team do it, on such a tiny minuscule budget?

By thinking out of the box!

The team started to make handmade 3D gre a patients using recycled paper. They also used colou s cotton buds to design the cards.

This way, they were able to save on many expenses, while the ingenuity of their actions rec of positive feedback. But the thing that drew a lot feedback from both the patients and the hospital ma was the heart and sincerity behind the actions.

The customer service team was able to prove a maj in customer satisfaction: the thought behind the action ma but the thougt would not have been significant without act bring it to reality.

Somehow, several companies often overlook these thi even in our world today. And at the end of everything, it the little small that build up to amazing customer experienc From the intricacies of a hand-folded card to remembering th name of a customer – it's the little things that led our customer satisfaction levels to skyrocket.

This is the result that happens when you empower your people.

In this case and many others, I granted my Head of Customer Service and other staff members full rein to do whatever was needed to create

"Wow moments" for our customers - as long as they worked within our principles.

As long as we are authentic to our customers and colleagues, driven with a strong work ethic to generate results, I generally allow my employees to operate with free will.

That's how I build collaborative relationships and add as much value as possible to the people I work with and the organization at large.

I stay open to ideas as much as possible to listen to suggestions nd provide feedback that can be used to make our ideas even ronger.

During and after each series of implementations, we meticulously review each action point to ensure that we were within compliance guidelines while meeting our expected goals.

This approach isn't only applied in the hospitals that I led, but also in other organizations that I've been a part of. These other organizations were not involved with hospital administration, but some dealt with drug trials, regulatory affairs, or medical devices.

And since this approach worked to great effect across various fields, I'm more than certain that applying even a portion of my strategies will create results that will result in great dividends for you and your brand.

Here's another quick example, based on research that analysed customer sentiment.

Studies tell us that customers tend to choose brands that make them feel at home.

In a hospital ward that looks nothing like a patient's house, it's these fine touches that help a patient feel warm, safe, and comforted.

That's why in the previous chapter, you read about how my staff took to decorating the ceilings and walls of our neonatal Intensive Care Unit with seasonal flourishes to create a playful and cheerful atmosphere, alleviating the critical condition of the patients.

If you are wondering about the level of customer service in your organization, you can start by answering a few questions:

Are you genuinely concerned about your customers?

How well do you show this concern?

What is the reception of your staff to queries and inquiries from customers?

Is your workplace ambience warm and friendly?

Does your organization show empathy for the customer when dealing with them?

Getting the best experience for your clients is not as hard as it seems.

It's the little things that build up to major impressions.

These little things often don't cost a fortune - they just need thougtfulness and genuine care.

It Has to Come from the Heart

One thing all exceptional customer care programmes have in common is that they come from the heart.

Companies often miss this critical mark. They make the customer care programme reactive rather than proactive—their customer service department spends more time fire-fighting, rather than building mutually beneficial relationships with their customers, like a particular pet supplies company.

Chewy is a company that takes care of pet supplies like food, toys, and medication. Marla Tabaka was one of their customers, and when her pet passed away, she shared her experience with Chewy, a company that takes care of Pets.

After her pet had been put to rest, she called Chewy to cancel her 'autoship' plan with them, an automated service that delivers supplies to customers.

Amazingly enough, the company was able to keep Marla as a customer even though she no longer had a pet.

And they did it by empathizing with her.

According to Marla, their response to her was very warm and comforting. It impressed her that they even got her name right. There had been other organizations that didn't spell her name right, and this meant a lot to her.

As a result of this heartfelt experience, she shared Chewy's response on social media and received comments affirming that others had similarly warm experiences with the pet food company as well. Others who never tried the service said they would look into it - and would most likely end up as customers for years, like Marla.

This is a simple example of how "zero cost" customer service is an important part of the most effective marketing strategies to retain your existing clientele and to attract new buyers into your fold.

Your commitment to ensuring optimal satisfaction for your clients should be sincere. And it starts with your organization committing to taking care of its staff—that's why we placed such a massive emphasis on employee care and engagement in the earlier chapters.

Treating customers right is a philosophy that's been proven to lead business success.

It can only happen when you treat your employees well. It needs to be a holistic approach

Thus, it is not surprising that companies with higher customer care ratings also tend to take care of their staff.

Artificial Intelligence (A.I.) is another means by which companies achieve customer satisfaction. Companies are beginning to understand the importance of A.I. and how it serves as a means to assess and ensure customer satisfaction when they use their products.

To date, Amazon continued to be one of the top customer-centric brands in the world. The reason was because the company had managed to integrate a customer care culture into the DNA of their employees.

Amazon CEO Jeff Bezos has been known to leave one seat open at the conference table.

When asked, he stated that the seat belonged to the "the most important person in the room – the customer".

Amazon is a brand that keeps appearing whenever the topic of customer satisfaction is brought up because the brand is highly reverent to its customers. This shows how much the brand takes customers' satisfaction into consideration, every step of the way.

Investing in the Thing That Matters

Once a company places importance on customer satisfaction, they are driven naturally by the sincere intention to help customers get the best experience.

But there is a balance to the art of serving customers.

Some companies try too hard to impress, which causes them to overlook the little things. These companies may invest in customer-focused software like expensive CRM (customer relationship management) and other digital tools which can be unnecessary—especially if they haven't ingrained customer service into the hearts and minds of their employees.

Instilling customer service as a core value is the thing that companies tend to forget - but it's the one thing that matters.

For instance, the world's best technology would not help the Chewy company with a grieving customer if their staff did not genuinely care about their customers. In Marla's report of her experience with Chewy, the first thing she stated about the brand was that it spelled her name correctly.

This piece of action might seem small to some people, but it certainly wasn't a minor thing to Marla.

From a customer service perspective, the most notable part of her story was that it did not cost the company anything to spell Marla's name right.

It is the same principle of how a simple and empathetic greeting can make customers fall in love with the brand... which is a zero-cost add-on to the products and services that you already sell.

Some companies spend millions of dollars on customer care, but end up wondering why their customers are rarely satisfied. If spent correctly, a big customer care budget can lead to spectacular results, but not if the company is missing the one thing that really matters...

The heart.

Leveraging and investing in the right technology can help boost customer satisfaction, just as Amazon showed us.

Many companies and management staff now use digital tools to obtain feedback from customers, which is a very cost-effective approach - but it must come from a genuine care for the people that you serve.

Getting on the Right "Ships"

It is important for companies to establish relationships with their customers. No matter how big the competition, customers would always choose brands they know.

The reason for this is that people feel safer with brands they can identify with.

This is why brands that make the customer like they are part of a big family achieve strong brand loyalty. Andrew Gazdecki, the CEO of BiznessApps stated:

"Your customers are living, breathing, emotive beings, not automatons, so play to their emotions.

If you treat customers with genuine courtesy and respect, they're far more likely to invest their faith in your business. And since customers put the food on the table, it shouldn't be hard to drum up some genuine appreciation for them".

He was talking about getting genuine customer care and service.

When trying to build a relationship with customers, these are a few things you might want to consider:

Obtain the details that matter

It is important to profile your customers in a holistic manner, because knowing the customer is essential for the decision-making process within your company.

Study the relevant data about the customers in your database. Make it a priority for your employees not to misspell customer names. For instance, birth dates, occupation, and other pertinent details are the details that have a major impact.

The home address of a customer is also important, especially for companies that include deliveries as part of their service.

Today, we are also dealing with a consumer-base that's more demanding than ever before. 72 per cent of customers expect companies to know their details and respond accordingly. This includes their contact details, product preferences, and service history.

Knowing your customers on a personal basis allows you to meet their needs better, but this means more responsibility and more work for your employees.

But if your company is genuinely concerned about customer satisfaction, it is something you will focus on and the results will speak for themselves in time to come.

Know Your Limits

It is also important to know the limits of a professional relationship and not cross them. Crossing these professional limits can come off as an intrusion of privacy to some customers.

It is very important that you instruct your frontline employees with the rules and processes that help maintain relationships with customers within professional standards.

Stay in Touch with the Customer

One way to maintain customer relationships is communication. It is important to ensure that as a company, you stay in touch with your customers.

This would help them know that you genuinely care about them.

As a matter of fact, companies should ensure that information flows to customers at timely intervals.

The communication should be open and honest.

Keeping your customers aware of developments within the company helps to gain their trust.

Although, most follow-up communication channels, especially the automated ones, are often not replied. This should not discourage companies from staying in touch with their customers.

Big brands like Amazon and Disney, understand the need for communication with customers, and this is one of the main reasons behind their success.

Handling Conflicts and Unsatisfied Customers

There are some cases of conflict that are not totally avoidable.

There would always be that small percentage of customers that are very hard to please. Sometimes, it's the grumpy patient in the hospital. Or the lady who nags a lot whenever she comes to shop in your store.

It is important to know the best approach to handling this category of customers so you can lead your team to do it well. Some basic, helpful steps are highlighted below.

➢ **Stay calm during the conversation:**

Customers in this category can sometimes be a handful. It is very easy to lose your temper and flare up when you are dealing with this customer type. So, the first thing to do is to maintain your cool as much as you can in the course of the conversation.

➢ **Ask questions and listen closely:**

Once you begin to engage these customers, pay close attention to them.

If there are any grey areas of the conversations present, try to ask as many questions as possible to obtain the necessary clarification. Customers want to know that you are listening to them, not just treating them as another problem to resolve.

➢ **Own up to your mistakes:**

In cases where the conflict is due to a mistake of the company, take full and complete responsibility. Anyone involved should also own up to the mistakes.

➢ **Negotiate and put in place a resolution:**

Once the source of the problem has been identified, you can proceed to reach an agreement with the client on the solution from that point. The resolution can be in the form of refunds, product replacement, or some sort of compensation agreeable to both parties.

➢ **Always say thank you:**

Always say "thank you" to your customers, irrespective of the circumstances or personalities involved.

If you do it right, you may be surprised at how easy it is to turn a "customer problem" into a "customer service opportunity"!

It goes without saying that providing your customers with the best experience at minimal cost to the company is not always easy.

And while you can approach customer service with minimal cost, remember that it is always about balance.

Balancing a mix of innovative "zero cost" efforts and pragmatic paid- for customer service programmes. Paying attention to how best to communicate and appreciate your customers.

Sometimes, thanking your customers lavishly can reap large rewards – we will talk about how a big budget can be put to good use in the next chapter.

All in All
(Learning Points)

- Ensuring the satisfaction of your customer is not just an excellent way to promote your brand, but also to build customer loyalty and business longevity.
- Achieving optimal customer satisfaction demands that the company builds a mindset towards it, reflecting genuinely in all the brand identity elements of the company with every employee developing a genuine concern for each customer that they serve.
- It's not about setting aside a large budget... Customer satisfaction is a mindset, not a number on the annual report. (In my hospital, my Head of Customer Service managed to skyrocket customer engagement and satisfaction levels - with a strict $500 budget!)
- Many customer service departments spend more time fire-fighting, rather than working on building mutually beneficial relationships with their customers.

CHAPTER 8 ▶▶▸

But Spare No Expense for the Customer

(When You Can Afford It)

Out of This World

On December 13, 2014, a particular rocket company launched their holiday party in Hawthorne, CA.

When a party requires a site plan and an indoor train—you read that right—that gives rides to guests around the entire party area, you know that the company is serious about giving their invitees an enjoyable time. This indoor train was called the SpaceXpress and you might have guessed it: the company is SpaceX.

To understand why SpaceX needed a site plan for their holiday party, we have to look at the number of rooms across their 2014 Christmas party.

There was a total of 12 rooms, with stops for riders to get on or off the SpaceXpress.

The party started with a check-in room to receive guests. After checking in their coats, they were promptly greeted by a massive SpaceX logo that was constructed and displayed exclusively on a wall of doughnuts.

From here, guests can wander off into one of the 12 rooms to get a snack, play, dance, or gamble. Each of these rooms were boldly labelled with capital letters.

There was a room filled waist-high with white plastic balls for everyone to relive their childhood again.

Surrounded by the train tracks was the Unclean Room, where guests can don a clean suit and proceed to paint a blank canvas or even the entire room, whichever way they please.

In a room marked as "Gamble", dealers dressed as Santarinas were waiting to deal poker cards and provide a night of Texas Hold'em entertainment.

In the centre of it all was a dark room, lit only with glow-in-the-dark acrylic foosball tables, a unique presentation on an otherwise regular table soccer experience.

There was even an entire room that was revamped with actual sand, beachballs, and surfboards to create an indoor shoreline in a room that was labelled as "Beach".

As a rocket company that pushes the boundaries of what is known to be possible in the realm of spaceflight, it goes without saying that SpaceX needed to win the hearts and minds of clients, investors, and employees alike.

And since every space launch costs tens to hundreds of millions of dollars, it is absolutely critical that clients and investors believe in the capabilities and work ethic of the team.

SpaceX employees are no strangers to working twelve hours or more per day, even staying overnight to get things done. They would tell you that no one forced them to contribute at this level, and they did so because they loved their work and are self-driven people who are extremely passionate about their company's mission.

I think you and I can both agree that SpaceX spared no expense in their parties.

Could this be how a company can attract not just clients and investors, but also top tier talent that work hard—and continue to remain diligent because they are taken care of and allowed to play hard too?

'Go Big'

It pays to spend on your customers.

While many companies obsess about cutting costs, Tim Manners (author of *Relevance: Making Stuff That Matters*) shares his secret, which is spending money where 'bean counters' would not.

If you feel resistive about costs, he says that:

"Spending extra money won't result in any extra sales, consider that it's not just about sales—it's about growth."

That said, it's not impossible to grow your business without spending a dime on their customers.

So why should you spend on your customers?

For one, think about the reason your company exists. You're in business because you can solve a problem that your customer is willing to pay you for.

Is that the only reason your customer should pay you?

What about the most successful companies, who have customers who are not just willing, but *happy* to part with their hard-earned cash?

Fans of Apple wouldn't think twice to pay for the latest iPhone, for example. They don't even consider a phone from any other manufacturer.

They are simply happy to buy the latest Apple product.

What if your company could attract this kind of following?

How much more revenue would your business gain?

How much more *growth* would your brand achieve?

These are the questions that I continually ask myself when we decide on purchasing equipment, designing spaces, and how my organization approaches customer service.

Do we make the 'traditional medical choice', or do we take a deeper look at what makes our patients truly happy?

At the end of the chapter, I'll be sharing more about how my management team and I achieved these customer service objectives to create the branding and growth that we wanted for our organization.

But first, we need to discuss why it is important to spend on your customers.

Spending on your customers should not be merely another cost in your expense report. It is one of the most important things your company can invest in for growth.

Unless you already own a monopoly for your market, I would strongly suggest that you take a closer look at what else you can do for your customers.

If you're not finding ways to make your customers' experience better, they might just go to competitors who have better customer service.

The most successful businesses never stop trying to make their customers smile, and continually pursue customer experience as a key focus.

If you are going to do something extra for your clients, go big!

Looking at the Returns

Keeping an eye on your ROI (return on investment) is important because it helps to consider the commercial reasons why and how your business should start implementing customer service efforts.

Investing in your customers requires planning, which lets you know what resources you need and how much you can afford to spend on customer experience.

You can start by either raising the quality of your goods and services, or reward your customers in the form of occasional dinner parties, gift vouchers, destination holiday vouchers, or a relevant incentive that's memorable and makes them run to your doors and not towards your competitors'.

As you begin to plan your customer service strategy, there is one more thing you need to keep in mind.

If you and five other companies provide a similar product or service, what makes your customer experience stand out?

More importantly, what reason do you give your clients to keep coming back, time after time?

The misconception that many companies have is that they think they constantly need new clients to grow the business. In chasing new clients, their current customers are left by the wayside.

Worse, they are forgetting that the primary source of growth for most businesses usually comes from repeat business from ***existing clients***.

Let's think about how this works.

If you treat your clients like lifelong partners and do everything in your power to maintain a cordial relationship with them, then they would be happy to pay you as often as they need your product or service.

They are also likely to bring you more customers by informing more people about your products and services because they are happy with what you're providing, and they want their friends to experience the same thing.

It eventually becomes word-of-mouth marketing, at no monetary cost to you.

So instead of ignoring them, it's usually best to ensure that they're completely satisfied first... before you try to find new clients!

When it comes to sales, the Harvard Business Review published research confirming that the chances of a business succeeding at selling to an existing happy client is 14 times higher than trying to sell to a new client, or 1,400 per cent.

I believe it's so important that it's worth repeating:

You're 14 times more likely to close a sale with an existing client who is happy with your company.

If you need to approximate the potential ROI that you can expect if you are planning your customer service efforts, that's a number you can keep in mind.

Now, we still have to find new customers, so it's a balance we must find—to budget an appropriate investment in maintaining relationships with current customers, and to set aside a fitting amount for finding new customers.

The Best Experience You Can Provide

Whether your budget is $1,000 or $100,000, the determining factor for the success of your customer service efforts is how you can create the most memorable experiences for your clients.

This is the most important thing in customer experience because your efforts here can go a long way.

And when it comes to customer experience, Southwest Airlines knows a thing or two about keeping their passengers happy.

Vicky Chase was a Southwest customer who was taking her 86-year-old mother via the airline to see the Latin pop singer Chayanne in Las Vegas.

The elderly lady was an enthusiastic fan of the musician, and it was her lifelong dream to see him perform.

Vicky and her mother reported early to their gate, but their growling stomachs sent them searching for a bite. Upon returning, they realized that to their great dismay, they had taken too long and their flight had already left.

It was time for Plan B.

They found other flights for Las Vegas, but those last-minute tickets cost at least $1,000, which were too expensive for the mother-daughter duo.

Vicky was very disappointed, feeling that she had let her mother down.

In low spirits, her tears were about to fall from her eyes as she explained her plight to a concerned Southwest Airlines employee named Christy.

Christy listened carefully to their story and told them that she would take care of them, and they will be enjoying the concert soon.

Christy generously offered them two of her employee "buddy passes", which meant that they were able to take a flight to Las Vegas for free to watch the concert.

Vicky and her mother were overwhelmed by the generosity of the employee and they went as far as sharing the exceptional customer experience with the TV station News4.

"We want to thank Christy, a Southwest employee at the Nashville International Airport, for her generosity.

Thank you for your kindness, for your love, and for helping me to fulfil my 86-year-old mother's dream," Vicky said.

"Southwest Airlines, you have a wonderful employee. She genuinely cares about people and her customer service skills were impeccable."

Hers is but one out of many stories about Southwest's legendary customer service.

If a story like Vicky's experience made a few people decide to become a Southwest customer, imagine what the hundreds of such accounts did for Southwest's branding and sales.

What would similar stories do for your business?

How many people would be convinced to become a new customer?

How many existing customers would be reaffirmed to stay on as your loyal customer, for years to come?

I hope that by now, you'd realize that making your customers happy does not necessarily require you to invest millions.

It just requires the heart.

In fact, no amount of money can create positive branding without the right intention behind it (just think of seven-figure advertisement campaigns that didn't earn any new customers for the advertiser).

Customers engage more in companies when the customer experience is outstanding, not because the company spent a fortune on advertising.

It's all about how your company treats your customers. If your budget is large, throw them a party to appreciate them, or send them gifts.

But no matter the size of your budget, deliver your customer service with the best attitude possible, just like Christy the generous Southwest employee did.

The 'wow' factor that your customer needs starts with a committed team with a well-organized system and leadership.

A Patient's First-Hand Experience

"I disembark from my car with ease, onto my wheelchair.

Wheeling into Farrer Park Hospital, my spirits are immediately alleviated by the gentle floral scent wafting in the air. It reminds me of the aroma of a hotel or a posh shopping mall.

Greeted by warm smiles from the counter staff in the spacious lobby area, I am happy that my check-in is fast and without hiccups.

I swoosh past the sliding doors into the medical centre, pleasantly surprised by the dimmed violet lighting at the lift waiting area.

My imminent medical procedures do not seem quite as intimidating anymore."

As a private tertiary healthcare establishment, we at Farrer Park Hospital pride ourselves in ensuring that our clients get the best care and treatment.

The hospital was designed from the ground-up by healthcare practitioners to deliver a patient-centric healthcare experience.

Our care philosophy extends beyond healing and the management of disease, to engaging patients as partners in the pursuit of good health.

It's common but not exactly pleasant that most hospitals smell like disinfectant. At Farrer Park, we knew it was very important to be different.

We sought to improve patients' experience and lightened their moods by greeting them with a gentle floral scent instead.

We are the first medical and hospitality complex to have machine-sterilized beds that ensure that the beddings are always clean.

The beds were imported from Germany and are washable and waterproof. Ordinary hospital beds usually undergo a wipe down after a patient's discharge. Our waterproof beds are different, with an automatic and thorough process that provides better infection control.

Our mattresses also feature the Micro-Stimulation Active System to enhance blood circulation while patients are resting.

The automatic beds also have a strict configuration process for infection control. With both heat and chemical sterilizations, the process is guaranteed to be effective.

"I decided to venture out to soak up some sun in the gardens.

I smile as the sun rays warm my skin, and I take in the vibrant colours of the fruits and vegetables planted in neat rows.

My nose tingles in delight at the light aroma emanating from the herbs growing alongside.

Guessing it being a good time for a bath, I head back to my hospital suite, and discover the shower area has a bench with a cut-out.

"Great! No need to go through the embarrassment of having the nurses to assist me," I thought gratefully."

An organization focused solely on profits may not have invested so much on the latest equipment or carved out green spaces, but we have carved out 15 gardens at multiple levels throughout the facility so that patients and families can have places to feel the warmth of the sun and breathe fresh air whenever they like.

The green space includes The Farm@Farrer, which grows fruits, vegetables and herbs, used specially for the preparation of patient meals.

Take a look at our design, architecture, and equipment, and I believe that you can see that our patients experienced how we spared no expense to ensure our facilities match their preferences and comfort levels.

We are keen to ensure that our facilities and equipment are meticulously designed to maximize comfort and efficiency while promoting our patients' well-being, rest, and recovery.

Even our carpark lots are expanded to 1.5 times the size of a standard lot, so we can welcome patients on crutches to comfortably extend the car door fully to disembark.

In the end, our decision to procure the best for our patients resulted in a branding that few organizations and even fewer hospitals can claim.

"Relaxing comfortably in my hospital bed after my treatment, I am kept occupied by the array of activities available on my personal tablet, attached on a convenient adjustable stand.

Top priority is placing my meal order, and I am spoilt for choice.

I was reassured by my doctor that all ingredients related to my food allergies have been removed, and each of my 6 meals spread throughout the day would be below 600 calories."

It took years to get to where we are today, but we can proudly say that we are a Singapore private hospital that offers excellent clinical care in unparalleled comfort, with a focus on fairness and value.

If a patient wants the best that medical advances can offer but with the comfort and service standards of a six-star hotel, Farrer Park Hospital is the place that they can trust to deliver.

Every department is equipped with the latest modern facilities, which allow us to diagnose, inform, and heal our patients, all with a seamless approach and friendly smiles from our medical professionals.

In the previous chapter, we spoke about how customers choose brands that make them feel at home.

While we provide the highest standards that a hospital can provide, we never allow our high standards to become a barrier between ourselves and our patients.

We are committed to creating a warm and welcoming atmosphere that's close to feeling as if they are home away from home.

We place a large emphasis on remembering our patients' birthdays, needs, and desires. While many organizations (especially some luxury brands) keep themselves distant from their customers, we want to be as close as possible to the people we serve.

"After a successful operation, all I have left to do is to recuperate.
I am transferred to the 5 Star hotel integrated within Farrer Park's Connexion complex. I'm glad for this option of a cheaper, yet comfortable recovery in a hotel.
The relocation is smooth and contained within the grounds of the complex, relieving the need to face the hustle and bustle of the outdoor traffic.
Knowing that my doctor is just minutes away, my mind is at ease as I sink into the plush covers of my bed for a good and confortable rest."

– A Patient's Account by Asia Pacific Biotech News (APBN)

While we still have much to grow, we will continue our journey while focusing on excellence in our care and service levels, always believing in value for quality clinical care at fair prices.

The ultimate aim is to boost good patient outcomes not just for Farrer Park Hospital, but across the industry.

We need to breakthrough by disrupting the norm, and one reason why we have consistently succeeded in disrupting the norm is through learning from others strategically, and that's a topic for the next chapter.

All in All
(Learning Points)

- The trick to giving the best customer experience is by having a strong focus on creating highly memorable customer experiences that earns you loyal clients that rave about you to anyone that would listen.
- Without the right focus and proper planning, spending on the clients could cause more harm than good. Therefore, spare no expense only when you have the right intentions and a solid strategy.
- The best customer experience is not the most expensive one, but the one done with the right heart, attitude, and intention.
- Even if the immediate returns are not large, investing in customer experience is important because in the long run, you will reap massive dividends.
- Spending on the customer also means giving them the best products and the best services. Therefore, it is as important to make sure that your products are of the best quality.

CHAPTER 9

Learning from the Best

Hospitality-Integrated Healthcare

A concierge service, personalized ensuite facilities, a bathroom complete with premium toiletries, and exceptional service from all the staff.

These are just a few of the many perks that a 47-year-old business owner enjoyed at Farrer Park Hospital (let's call her Ms. Lim). She was there for only five nights, but her experience made her feel as if she was at home.

One of the highlights of her stay was how the staff went the extra mile to provide her with cranberry juice. This might sound almost insignificant to some of you, but it was highly relevant and sorely desired by Ms. Lim.

Why did this seemingly minor detail hold such importance to the staff of Farrer Park and Ms. Lim herself?

Think, if you would, of an avid golfer. A reactive resin bowling ball, no matter how premium, would be of minimal interest. A high-end titanium golf driver, would not only hold attention, but create an endless stream of conversation, even if the said golfer was an introvert.

It's all about relevance.

The cranberry juice was not on the menu, but she loved drinking it as a complimentary herbal remedy for her ailment all the same.

The juice was highly relevant to her.

She said it reminded her of her childhood days, and it made her look forward to her meals, brightening her entire experience.

She was already feeling very uncomfortable because she was admitted for a renal condition that required intravenous treatment. The facilities and the hospitality of the staff made her feel as if she was in a five-night 'stay-cation.'

When asked about her experience, Ms. Lim said, "I was so comfortable, I felt as if I was in a five-star hotel."

Seeing as we were the first fully-integrated healthcare-hospitality complex in the country, I can assure you that the work it took to bring about such customer experiences did not happen overnight.

With Singapore's exceptional patient services and dedication to innovation, we remain as the best destination for those seeking medical care. By providing convenience, comfort, and value in our medical sector, there is no doubt that it will continue to expand and grow.

However, in such a competitive environment, getting the upper hand in this industry is not easy.

Singapore is a multifaceted medical hub and a centre of excellence.

Patients here receive an excellent standard of medical treatment, comparable to that in Europe and America. However, staying on top of the pyramid is not easy.

It takes perseverance work and exceptionally synchronized services to make our clients feel valued.

Currently, we are attracting foreign patients who expect a five- or six- star hotel service, because we are a private hospital. One of our 'secrets' for staying at the top is cross-training, which has played a key role in helping us improve our services in more ways than one.

But it's not just us.

Other top-tier companies also use this cross-expertise training to increase the effectiveness of their employees and maintain their position as industry leaders.

External Cross-Training with the Ritz

In the early 2000s, there were no hospitals that one would call six-star in Singapore, but there was one six-star hotel.

You've read it before in previous chapters; it's the Ritz-Carlton – the brand that's recognized as one of the best hotels in the world.

"On our way to bed, we took a pre-bedtime stroll and we walked close to the banks of the river. It was so close that it was just a step right out of the hotel.

There were chiselled stepping stones that lead to the Kamo River. Just before getting there, we passed the famous stone boat sculptures that decorated the hallway.

All this follows the previous day's amazing tour of the city. We were 318 miles away at Ritz-Carlton's gleaming midtown tower.

Nonetheless, the staff enthusiastically connected us with everything in Tokyo. We went to see exotic historical discoveries and enjoyed the street-food-themed visit to the Ritz-Carlton in Osaka.

The staff seemed to know what we wanted even before we asked for it.

In the short time my son and I were in the hotel, we were treated like royalty. I cannot compare the ambience and the reception I got to any other hotel I have ever been to."

This is one of hundreds, if not thousands of positive feedback that Ritz guests give the hotel, which always speak of their legendary service and 6-star experience.

To be the best, you have to learn from the best.

If my hospital were to define itself and stand out from the other organizations in the medical industry, we couldn't keep learning from within ourselves - we needed to look outside and defer to a cross—industry perspective.

We expected to the best in the hospitality industry, and we found the Ritz - hence the external cross-training that we undertook.

That was, and still is, my steadfast belief.

To find ways to transform the hospital into the best possible version it could be, I took the initiative to collaborate with the CEO of Ritz-Carlton for the cross-attachment training.

Since the Ritz is among the best companies in the hospitality industry, I knew that we could learn much from them.

As a result, the initiative to cross-train with them gave a significant boost to many of our capabilities and services.

We borrowed their models on what they did to get to the top and what they practised every day to remain there.

Cross-training allowed our employees to grow their emotional and intellectual skills that have developed to a significant performance factor.

We believed that to rise to the top, we have to look as groomed, we need to be as personable, like those in hospitality and the airlines.

As previously mentioned in Chapter Two, cross-training with the Ritz helped us create and polish various corporate practices. The training was instrumental in improving our ***management performance, establishing a lasting and evolutionary corporate culture, improving our hospitality, increasing our range of products and services, and the empowerment of our customers and employees (the 'Wow' experience).***

Since our cross-training bore fruits, we opened up to help others as well.

Through opening up our organization, we were able to offer others the same opportunity we were given to make a global mark in the industry.

Our hospital serves as a teaching site at Nanyang Technological University. We are in collaboration with their medical faculty, the Lee Kong Chian School of Medicine.

The board of directors sought the help of private organizations like ours to support the infrastructure of the Singapore healthcare and capacity building.

We designed a teaching clinic, a lecture theatre, seminar rooms, and large conference facilities. This will give the students of the medical school an opportunity to attend classes organized at our hospital. They will be able to receive firsthand lessons from our specialists at the hospital who were appointed as academic clinical lecturers.

The learning courses included beaming live tutorials obtained directly from the operating rooms and special medical seminars held at the hotel ballroom, which is seamlessly integrated with the hospital.

This way, the students are able to learn the skills, advancements, and revolutionary changes in the industry.

Internal Cross-Training: Cross-Functionality

Employee productivity at Peace River Pulp is among the highest in their industry.

They have been operating a pulp and paper manufacturing business since 1989, and they are consistently recognized for being a top employer in Canada.

The company celebrates and attributes this achievement to its *crossfunctional team system*, which means that the teams within the company are set up with members who possess different functional expertise (finance, marketing, operations, and human resources departments).

Their success proves that cross-training can benefit companies not just externally, but also *internally*.

For one, Peace River Pulp managed to keep worker-idleness to the absolute minimum with the help of internal cross-training, and even allows the company to keep a 'minimum-staff strategy'.

Where other companies struggle with redundancies and headcount bloat, Peace River Pulp operates on only the least number of operators required, lowering costs and maximizing productivity.

The pulp and paper company runs a 'continuous production system', an operational framework which does not divide jobs into individual pieces.

Rather than segregating each part of the job, workers are cross-trained to be proficient about different parts of the process, so they can serve as multi-faceted engineers.

A Peace River Pulp employee functions like a Swiss army knife, as opposed to just another one-dimensional 'cog in the machine'.

According to their management, this programme has improved their decision-making structure, production, and even work satisfaction.

In their internal cross-training, they prefer to avoid written job descriptions or policies when it comes to sharpening their employees. This is because they want to avoid constraining the flexibility of the organization.

Having observed the breakthrough results of cross-training, many other companies seeking to increase productivity and flexibility have turned to cross-training programmes to increase the skills of their workers.

Advanced Cross-Training: Cross-Mentoring

Cross-mentoring is the exchange of mentors and mentees between companies in different industries.

Over time, there has been a rise in cross-mentoring models in both large and small corporations, where the flow of mentoring and training can be one-sided or reciprocal.

Sometimes the exchange happens under the supervision of a professional body, for example, the *UK Institute of Practitioners*. The board of this organization initiates advertising programmes that link young entrepreneurs of advertising agencies with more experienced companies.

This significantly improved the company culture of the business that enforced growth.

In the same way, the Chartered Institute of Personnel and Development also created a project that linked highly experienced Human Resource directors with aspiring HR directors across different companies.

One of the first-ever documented cases of cross-mentoring was the Irish Post Office. The office was planning on launching an ambitious programme to support career advancement for women in middle and junior management.

Unfortunately, the initiative was concluded due to the lack of sufficient potential mentors within its senior executives. As a result, the office reached out to its supply chain for help.

It incorporated the help of some of its biggest customers and suppliers, asking them to provide them with mentors.

A similar situation happened in a large UK-based bank.

The bank wanted its regional directors to become more 'commercially aware'. While the company had great banking skills, their perception of the business was limited. Therefore, it sought mentors from a range of customer-centric businesses, including McDonald's.

Consequently, the directors attended a training programme that improved the area in which they were lacking.

When it comes to leadership growth in your company, cross-mentoring is an essential element.

A popular example of a cross-mentoring training programme is the 'six companies- mentoring initiative'.

In this model, each company provides two mentees and two mentors.

The 12 mentees are then divided into two sections.

Each division works on one issue for each of its members and shares accountability for the outcomes.

After they find the results, they present them to the sponsors together.

In most cases, the sponsors are the CEOs of the various companies.

This alliance of mentoring and action-based learning is a powerful method that speeds up and accelerates the growth of leadership capabilities among several companies.

In cases where there is no organization supervising the development of the cross-mentoring, mentors and mentees are encouraged to set up peersupport groups to maintain and keep up their momentum.

No matter what model is used, cross-mentoring generally requires all arrangements to begin and end formally. When an arrangement eventually reaches a conclusion, mentees can find a mentor from another company to pursue growth in a particular skill set.

All in All
(Learning Points)

- Cross-training is the systematic process of training employees to perform their work and be able to understand their inter-department counterparts better. For it to be effective, it must be carried out both vertically and horizontally throughout the business.
- Cross-training can be arranged externally, internally, and even in the form of cross-mentoring.
- Cross-training provides variety for your employees' work experience and provides operational readiness. Ultimately, this produces a happier and more productive workforce.
- Interaction between companies allows your staff to be more aware of what other employees are doing outside their scope. This builds a sense of teamwork within and between employees.
- Subordinates and lower-ranking employees need cross-training just as much as managers do. When leaders are upgraded through cross-training, they become more valuable to their corporations with newfound skills, which leads to job enrichment for themselves and the people that they lead.
- Cross-mentoring can be a highly effective strategy that adds value in creative ways that would be almost impossible within their respective industries. Mentor-mentee support in programmes between different companies can help your employees equip themselves with skills that they wouldn't be able to acquire otherwise.

CHAPTER 10 ▶▶▶

Giving Back

The Need to Give Back

It goes without saying that organizations need to make a profit. We need to keep operations lean and expenses low. However, when your organization has reached a certain amount of growth, it's time to think about giving back to the community and earning the goodwill of customers (current and future).

Most organizations don't consider giving back to be important, especially when it doesn't have any immediate benefits for the organization.

Many business managers and company boards may even avoid 'give back' activities, aiming only to include profit margins and ROI.

As an organization, it is not always easy to make the choice to give back.

Depending on your current organizational practices, it may even be an immense challenge to justify why you should do it.

But giving back can be more helpful than one might think—research tells us that giving back actually does more good than harm for your business (more on this later).

Often, companies give back only as a means to only fulfil CSR (Corporate Social Responsibility) requirements. Some governments mandate companies to carry out CSR projects, and companies may just comply for the sake of complying.

And if you are only 'giving back' as an obligation, people (especially your customers) can feel the lack of authenticity and sincerity.

That's why it is more important to give back with a high level of sincerity.

Giving back should not be because the government enforces CSR, but because you genuinely care for your customers and community.

It is also interesting to note that the preferences of consumers are evolving. These days, consumers are more likely to pick a brand that exists for a higher purpose than to make a profit.

One of the ways to demonstrate your higher purpose is by giving back in a way that is in-line with your vision and mission, and when done right, this can lead to massive commercial success for you and your company.

But before we get to commercial success, we need to talk about or discuss what practical research studies prove to us.

Giving back can occur in many forms. Let's start with the obvious ones.

Donating money to charity or non-profit organizations is a form of giving back. Volunteering for community projects or offering your services at a lower cost or for free to disadvantaged people are other ways to give back.

Studies also confirm that the youth prefer organizations with a 'giving back mentality'.

In a 2017 research study published by Cone Communications, a Boston based agency focusing on corporate social responsibility and brand communications confirmed these significant trends when it came to younger consumers.

Millennials were found to be 87 per cent more willing to purchase a product with a social or environmental benefit. about CSR efforts, and 74 per cent more inclined to volunteer for a cause

This demographic is also 82 per cent more likely to tell friends and family supported by a company they trust.

The research went even further to determine how far the younger generation would go.

They also found that millennials are prepared to make personal sacrifices to make an impact on issues they care about– whether that's paying more for a product (70 per cent), sharing products rather than buying (66 per cent) or taking a pay cut to work for a responsible company (62 per cent).

People want companies that not only tell us what they sell, but what they *stand for*, and giving back is a great place to start.

Encouraging a mentality of giving back is important in your organization. If you can inspire your staff to find ways to be more connected to your customers and give back to society, you may find a marked increase in performance as a result of a more fulfilling work experience through giving back.

Customers also have a higher tendency to choose your products and services over competitors if they can associate the emotions of your CSR efforts with your brand. When your company has reached this level of emotional impact, customers feel a need to give back to your brand (through doing business with you or advocating your work), and it becomes a cycle of giving back.

This creates a virtuous cycle of goodwill.

Companies that encourage their workers to give back have a more fulfilled workforce, particularly the ones that volunteer for projects in their local communities.

Giving Back at Farrer Park Hospital

At Farrer Park Hospital (FPH), giving back is a major part of our work.

It might not be in the form of substantial monetary donations. But to us, our CSR projects give back the same, if not higher, value.

Two of the most notable ways in which we give back to our society include our educational programmes, and helping people in need.

Our Partnership Education Programmes

At FPH, we have partnership programmes to help medical students, particularly in the course of their programme.

FPH is one of the first private hospitals to be heavily involved in undergraduate medical training, partnering with the Lee Kong Chian School of Medicine (a medical school of the Nanyang Technology University in Singapore). The medical school uses FPH as a teaching site for their students.

Our education programmes at Farrer Park Hospital is one example of how we give back to the community.

Helping People in Need

Another way we give back is by keeping an eye out for patients and finding the best way to help them.

We understand that not everyone can afford expensive treatments.

Some of these expensive procedures are sometimes needed in treatment.

Another challenge we found was that patients do not understand the nature of their conditions.

At Farrer Park Hospital, we run free diagnostic procedures and treatment for underprivileged communities. This helps us to confirm their medical condition and allows us to work out the most efficient treatment plan without breaking the bank.

For instance, a 71-year-old woman (we'll address her as Madam LHK) had some difficulties in reading for a while. It was due to a cataract that had affected her left eye for 6 years.

Madam LHK was a retiree and not being able to read was a tremendous distress to her quality of life.

She was also a regular at the Pek Kio Community Centre in Singapore, an organization that we'd reached out to as part of our Free Cataract Surgery efforts. Madam LHK benefited from the scheme and has had amazing eyesight since, thus regaining her quality of life.

When speaking to the press, an overjoyed Madam LHK stated, "I can see fine print from a shorter distance after the surgery." She also expressed intense appreciation for her surgeon.

Madam LHK was one of three elderly patients to enjoy free surgery at the time. Two other beneficiaries were also regular members of the Pek Kio Community Centre.

The Free Cataract Surgery was a part of our CSR efforts at Farrer Park Hospital, which was started by eye surgeon Dr Bobby Cheng. Before this CSR initiative, FPH also helped some elderly residents at the Jamiyah Home for the Aged, two years before Madam LHK's surgery.

We understand that there are still many patients who cannot afford cataract surgery. The cost of the surgery is currently at about S$6,500 on average.

On top of the high cost, many underprivileged patients may be unaware of their options and are afraid to take action. That's why we do it for free, to improve the lives of the beneficiaries of this scheme, complete with diagnostics and surgery.

Our efforts have continued to grow over time, with an increasing number of beneficiaries all over the country. To make the selection process efficient, we partner with local community centers so they can ensure that the most qualified beneficiaries are the ones we serve.

This way, we are sure that people who need the surgery the most are the ones that receive it.

We also enjoy support from some brands for our Free Cataract Surgery.

Some of these brands include; Zeiss, Bausch and Lomb and AMO. These brands donate most of the equipment and lenses that are needed for the surgeries.

The Free Cataract Surgery will not be the last time Farrer Park Hospital would be going out of its way to give back. One of the surgeons involved in the Free Cataract Surgery is Dr. Au Eong Kah Guan, who described the initiative as one that had its stresses, but it was ultimately very satisfying to be a part of this cause to benefit underprivileged communities.

It was a heartwarming endeavour that was a blessing for both surgeons and patients alike.

We're already planning to create more partnerships for CSR efforts like the Free Cataract Surgery, so that this initiative can grow and benefit even more people.

Why Giving Back Is Commercially Viable

Earlier, we mentioned that giving back can be tricky for companies.

Most executives may only be concerned with achieving maximum profits, but giving back can also have positive effects on your revenue as a company.

Let's go through the reasons that make it commercially give back to society as a company, before we get into a few case studies of multi-million companies.

Improve Relationships with Customers

It is important to find ways to make your company stand out, especially if you're in a competitive market.

You can try to lower your prices to make customers choose your product over others, but will they stay loyal to you? Or would they stop buying from you if a cheaper option comes along?

One way to stand out without sacrificing your margins is by giving back.

Most customers remain loyal to a brand when the brand offers more than a product or a service. Giving back to your society gives your customers a feeling that you care about causes other than just profits.

This can help improve your relationship with your old customers, and will help you win you new ones.

Customers See Philanthropy as Positive and Empathetic

When people see your company giving back to the community, they are more likely to do business with you, compared to if you did not stand for a cause.

Previously, we discussed how millennials were 87 per cent more willing to purchase a product with a social or environmental benefit.

In a separate research study, the same company carried out a study that revealed that 82 per cent of the consumers surveyed consider a brand's amount of CSR when they shop.

Two major demographic classes considered in the study were mothers and millennials.

If your target market involves young adults or women, then it's even more important to invest more into your CSR efforts.

Your Employees are Happier and More Purposeful at Work

Giving back is an ideal that should be well rooted in the foundation of a company.

Encourage the members of your staff to not see giving back as a compulsory segment of their job, but as a part of advancing your organization's overall vision.

As business owners and managers, we need to support our employees with a "give back" mentality, and you can achieve this by encouraging them to volunteer and participate in community projects.

More and more young professionals prefer organizations that allow them to give back to their society. By encouraging employees to give back, they are likely to have a happier and more fulfilled work experience.

Companies that Give Back

➢ CarMax

CarMax is the United States' largest used-car retailer and a Fortune 500 company.

Over the years, CarMax has caused a revolution in the auto industry, after starting operations over 25 years ago. CarMax has been able to achieve this by delivering optimal service.

They offer honest, transparent and trustworthy car buying experiences to their customers. CarMax is still able to stay relevant in the auto industry due to the innovative vision of the CarMax brand, with over 195 stores around the country and using modern technology to make the process of acquiring a car very convenient. Essentially, they removed the uncomfortable bargaining process from purchasing a used car.

Apart from their success in the auto industry, CarMax is recognized widely for giving back.

The company established the CarMax Foundation, which is committed to helping communities, particularly communities where CarMax associates work and live. The foundation has helped a lot of CarMax staff to give back by integrating their team-building processes and CSR efforts to increase the impact of their work.

The CarMax Foundation also provides financial donations to eligible non-profits, in areas such as education, youth leadership, and children's healthy living through their larger grant programme.

➢ Equinox

Equinox offers health and fitness facilities to its members, with each of their locations equipped with premium fitness facilities. Members have access to gym equipment, spa, and even a shop with Equinox branded apparel. They are also able to choose from a range of classes to improve their fitness levels.

Expert trainers are also available for members to receive coaching and work towards maximizing their potential.

Outside of their work in the fitness sphere, Equinox also raises money for cancer research. This is one example of how they give back to society.

Equinox is also a founding partner of The Heroes Project, which cares for injured war veterans. A beneficiary of this project is Marine Staff

Sergeant Charlie Linville. Through Equinox's CSR efforts, Sergeant Linville became the first combat-wounded veteran to reach the top of Everest.

- **Greenpac**

Greenpac provides customized eco-friendly packaging to a diverse range of companies, including Fortune 500 firms.

This company's business model and operations were founded entirely on social responsibility, starting with how they specifically source for environmentally sustainable materials. They develop unique packaging solutions that are collapsible, reusable and returnable so that their clients can reduce waste and reduce costs.

The firm believes in inclusive hiring, employing disabled workers and subcontracts certain projects to ex-offenders under the Yellow Ribbon Project initiative. Their business model also includes a comprehensive workplace health and safety system.

Greenpac is the proud owner of Singapore's first "green factory", featuring a solar panel rooftop and state-of-the-art, energy-efficient technologies. Singapore's Deputy Prime Minister and Finance Minister

Tharman Shanmugaratnam commended the firm as an example of how it is possible to pursue commercial profits while contributing to a better environment and social well-being.

From a one-woman operation in 2002, Greenpac and its socially responsible vision has since grown into a multimillion-dollar company today.

➢ Singapore Press Holdings

Singapore Press Holdings (SPH) is a media organization in Singapore with businesses predominantly in print, digital, radio and outdoor media.

SPH has an employee base of over 4,000 that comprises 1,000 journalists and correspondents operating around the world.

Their CSR efforts are equally expansive, covering arts, charity, community, education, sports, and conservation causes.

From lending support to help disadvantaged children develop their artistic talents to offering free concerts to the public throughout the year through the annual SPH Gift of Music series, SPH's diverse range of programmes have reached out to various groups of the community and made a difference in many lives.

SPH also donates to over 20 charities, raises funds to help underprivileged children, and organizes many other events to benefit the community.

All over the world, companies give back to their societies in different ways.

It doesn't always mean that you have to make multi-million-dollar donations to charities to make a difference. Sometimes, it can be in the little things, like helping to paint a community facility or donating items to an orphanage.

Giving back can be in ways other than monetary donations, you just have to find a way that suits your company the best.

Feedback Is Important

Giving back is important in the trajectory of any company's success.

Most of the larger companies in the world today have projects that give back to society. If they're doing it, then it should be important for your company too, big or small.

It is also important to ensure that your efforts in giving back is effective - you can use metrics such as customer feedback, number of visits to your website or physical stores, and even ask your employees about their opinion!

This way, you are sure that your investment has a real impact on society and does not end up as a 'white elephant' project that helps no one.

A way to achieve this is through the promotion of your project. Tell more people about it on your website, on social media channels, and in publications. After all, if you're giving back, I'm sure your customers (current and future) will want to know!

What I've also discovered is that an effective CSR programme is a way for companies to express gratitude for the communities that they serve. It is a form of blessing to others, and it's more than likely that these companies will be blessed right back.

There's an old African proverb that goes, *"If you want to go fast, go alone. If you want to go far, go together."*

We couldn't have done it all on our own. As a company, we need people we can trust internally to function. We need external parties like customers and shareholders to grow our revenue.

In following this concept, the next chapter will talk about how a solitary visionary cannot stand alone, and neither can a single operator, no matter how talented one may be.

All in All
(Learning Points)

- Companies who give back tend to inspire customers to give back to them (in the form of sales); it's a virtuous cycle of goodwill.
- Giving back is not only a means to fulfil CSR (Corporate Social Responsibility) requirements. Truly giving back

can help boost a company's revenue through unexpected ways.

- ✦ People want companies that not only tell us what they sell, but what they stand for, and giving back is a great place to start demonstrating what your company believes in, and gives a reason for people to do business with you.
- ✦ Giving back is commercially viable because it improves your relationships with customers, makes them feel that your company is positively empathic, and gives your employees purpose and fulfilment.
- ✦ If big companies like Carmax and Greenpac are giving back and finding success, then every company should too!
- ✦ Giving doesn't have to be monetary—it can be service-based as well.

CHAPTER **11**

Every Visionary Needs An Operator

Thinkers and Doers

At the most basic level of organizations, we have "thinkers" and "doers".

That is not to say that some people are only one or the other. A manager might be more of a thinker, but less of a doer. An employee may be the reverse; more of a doer than a thinker- but our strengths generally lie in one or the other.

The Thinker-Doer classification of personalities is one that has existed for decades. The 'thinker' is a person that prefers to think an activity through before taking any action.

Thinkers have a wonderful mind and are often curious and clever. They are very good at analyzing situations. Yet, this ability to 'think' is both the strength and weakness of Thinkers.

They often tend to be more laid back when it comes to taking action. This is where the Doers come in.

Doers have a more carefree attitude than Thinkers. They tend to jump into the execution phase without fully thinking things through. Not thinking things through sometimes could lead to undesirable outcomes.

To successfully execute an idea, we need a balance of both personalities.

And to achieve great outcomes in any company, you will require a symmetry of both thinkers and doers.

In the organizational structure, the CEOs are the visionaries in most cases.

They are the ones who conceive the fundamental ideas behind the organization and are often able to picture innovations in the organization before others. This trait makes most CEOs fall under the 'thinker' personality.

They are responsible for becoming the embodiment of the company's vision, mission, and core values—and to continually remind the organization of the dream that everyone is working towards, ad-infinitum.

As a thinker, visionary CEOs may face problems when it comes to execution, because few CEOs can balance the thinker-doer split. This is the reason why it is advisable to balance out the thinker personality of CEOs with a 'doer' COO.

The COO is the Chief Operations/Operating Officer of the company, holding one of the highest-ranking executive positions in an organization.

The COO is the one in charge of the day-to-day operations of the organization and is the "go to person" when it comes to getting things done. The COO is the 'doer'.

There are other roles that are responsible for 'thinking', just as there are 'doing' roles in every company, but for the sake of simplicity, let's establish the CEO as the 'thinker', and the COO as the 'doer'.

In organizational leadership, the Thinker-Doer duo is called the Visionary-Operator duo, based on the responsibilities involved. The CEO is in charge of coming up with innovations for the organization. The COO has to deal with the daily operations of the organization and find ways to execute the ideas from the CEO. Some organizations merge the CEO and COO positions, sometimes because they believe the person occupying the position can balance both roles. But we've established that very few people can handle the responsibilities of both thinking and doing the same time, so it is almost always advisable to separate both positions.

In this chapter, we'll be looking at real-life examples of this in action, from Farrer Park Hospital to Apple Inc. (In the next chapter, we will discuss a method—the AEM-cube—that makes it possible to assess and develop these positions, as well as other roles, within teams.)

Another advantage of separating these positions is higher specialization, so that each person can be more focused on their aspect of the work.

When the leaders of the organization are focused on what they do best, that's when you can achieve optimal results. The CEO's attention is concentrated on innovative solutions for the growth of the organization, while the COO optimizes day-to-day operations—that's how these roles can best work together to bring new ideas to reality.

In any company, it is important that the leaders understand this thinkerdoer concept, and set up an environment for everyone to excel.

More importantly, an idea is only as good as its execution.

That's why the thinkers of any organization need to share their ideas as clearly and as articulately as possible, while the doers execute the ideas as efficiently and accurately as possible.

Within a Hospital Context

An efficient visionary-operator pair is the secret behind the success of most organizations. Top companies in the world have an efficient visionaryoperator pair handling their affairs.

For instance, at Farrer Park Hospital, I play the role of the visionary.

But I cannot do my job alone. I need the support of the Director of Nursing and other key members of the hospital. With this, I can steer the affairs of the hospital towards the right direction successfully.

It's my job to understand the key issues of the hospital. I do this by walking the grounds regularly, observing patient-staff interactions, talking to both staff and patients, and noting down what the general sentiment is.

Where things can be improved, I bring up the problem and potential solutions to my management team.

At this point, I pass the baton to the departments in this management team. If it's a patient-related issue, my customer service department needs to step up and find a suitable solution. If it's a nursing staff related problem, then the nursing department needs to take note and resolve it.

I find that when you empower and trust people to do their work, they often surprise you - after all, they're the ones "on the ground" everyday - and they're more than capable of coming up with solutions, sometimes even better than I can. Some companies constrict their employees with a stranglehold, afraid to give them any leeway, but I find it more effective to treat them as you would a bird - free to fly and perform in their own capacity, but welcome to come back for rest and camaraderie at any time.

We need to lead our people with thoughtfulness and guide them with strong principles and a work ethic that generates results.

It's one thing to be in charge as a CEO, but it is another to foster a loyal following from your employees - and I found that the best way to earn loyalty is through collaboration, rather than trying to "over-control" others.

I've always thought of my role as one that's responsible for building a strong team and to increase the visibility and reputation of the organization.

After two years of regional awards (25 awards in 25 months), against other competitors in Asia Pacific, I'm proud to say that Farrer Park Hospital is en route upwards as one of the top healthcare providers in both Asia and the world.

In my tenure here, we groomed strong key appointment holders who hold important functions and continually benchmarked ourselves against the best airlines and hotels in the region, as far as service is concerned.

From opening the doors of Farrer Park Hospital in 2016 till today, there are many milestones that resonate with me. One of my proudest achievements is transforming and cultivating the service attitude of our staff, so that every patient that comes into our care can immediately experience the Farrer Park difference, professionalism, heart-felt kindness, and even our refined look and personal presentation.

At the end of the day, it is the feedback of our patients and care-givers that continues to drive me forward and maintain my people-oriented focus, no matter what the goals of the respective organizations are.

As vision-makers, we still need to be in touch with our operators and the rest of our management team.

I have been a part of different organizations, some in hospital administration, others in clinical trials, product development, medical affairs, or regulatory affairs.

In these different environments I attribute much of my success to coming down to the ground to be hands-on with the people that I lead—it matters not if I hold the title of Vice President, Regional Medical Director, or as the Chief Executive Officer.

Visionary-Operator Pairs That Turned Out Amazing!

➢ A Tale of Two Steves

Steve Jobs and Steve Wozniak are without a doubt, one of the most wellknown visionary-operator pairs of the late 20th and early 21st centuries.

They co-founded Apple in 1976, and at the time, they started in a space that is little more than a garage. A few decades later, Apple had grown into one of the biggest technology companies in the world— so much that

Apple achieved the title of becoming the first private-sector publicly traded company in the world to be valued at over a trillion dollars.

The early years of the company relied heavily on the partnership between Jobs and Wozniak. But even before they started Apple, Jobs and Wozniak were friends.

Jobs designed video games at Atari and Wozniak worked at Hewlett Packard, and the former would often come to Wozniak for help on the execution of his ideas. He would then share the bonuses from the video game sales with Wozniak afterward.

It was difficult for Jobs to handle complex projects alone, and that's why Wozniak, being a hardware and software guru, was such a great match.

This partnership would lead to the founding of Apple by the friends.

Computers at the time were big, intimidating machines that occupied large spaces and were complex to use, and the duo built a version that was smaller and more accessible to the average computer user. This machine would go on to become Apple I, quickly followed by its better-known successor: The Apple II.

But Jobs saw more than a simple computer. He saw bigger and better opportunities.

Jobs then went on to find ways to sell the computers. Wozniak would later say about Jobs:

"Steve didn't do one circuit, design, or piece of code," recalls Wozniak.

"But it never crossed my mind to sell computers.

It was Steve who said, 'Let's hold them up in the air and sell a few.'"

Jobs had the vision that no one else could see, not Hewlett-Packard (Wozniak's then-employer), not Atari (Job's then-employer), and not even the Wozniak himself.

After trying unsuccessfully to pitch their idea, they scraped together the funds that were needed to produce the original printed circuit boards for the computer.

In the years that followed, Jobs went on to become the face and personification of Apple, while Wozniak preferred a more private life.

Together, they developed the Apple I, Apple II, and the first commercial graphical user interface PCs, the Lisa, and the Macintosh (though Wozniak was only peripherally involved in the latter two).

And to give credit where credit was due, Jobs admits that he was "nowhere near as good an engineer as Woz."— a testament to how visionaries and operators cannot reach their full potential without each other's help.

The Jobs-Wozniak partnership is the quintessential story that illustrates how CEOs and COOs work best, told in a tale that resulted in the revolution of personal computers.

But what's one without the other?

Many people have argued that Jobs could have made it without Wozniak.

And on the other side, several technical men have also argued that Jobs needed Wozniak more. Ultimately, these arguments are just another two in the long list of comparisons of Visionaries and Operators. People ask who is more important.

The truth is that both are equally important. Jobs needed Wozniak and Wozniak needed Jobs. Wozniak came up with the technicalities, without which there would have been nothing to sell. But Jobs designed and sold the products. With each iteration, he came back with ideas on how to make the products better based on the needs of users.

Jobs was more than an efficient marketer; he was a visionary. This is why even now, years after his death, Apple is still going strong.

➢ Brian and Belinda (Airbnb)

Another Visionary-Operator pair of noteworthy mention would be Brian Chesky and Belinda Johnson of Airbnb. As an online marketplace, this company's main offering is hospitality service brokerage.

Most of us have used their massively successful platform to arrange or offer peer-to-peer lodging and tourism-based services. In the third quarter of 2018, the company announced a revenue of more than $1 billion.

At the helm of Airbnb, Brian Chesky sits as CEO and Belinda Johnson as the chief business affairs and legal officer.

Brian handles the innovation front of Airbnb, and is responsible for coming up with new plans for the growth and expansion of the company. Belinda is, of course, the operator that drives the company and is hailed as Airbnb's Sheryl Sandberg (more on this in the next few pages).

Belinda's previous work with other tech companies like AudioNet, Yahoo, and PayPal provided a solid base of experience and proficiency that helped to keep things running smoothly at Airbnb.

The consistent success of Airbnb shows the efficient leadership of the company, with Brian and Belinda as a model Visionary-Operator pair.

➢ Mark and Sheryl (Facebook)

Mark Zuckerberg and Sheryl Sandberg form another notable Visionary- Operator pair.

Sheryl was not part of the founding team of Facebook; she was vice-president at Google before joining Facebook, where she handled global online sales and operations.

Sheryl was listed among the 100 most influential people in the world by Time Magazine in 2012. She is known for getting things done, a reputation she has upheld proudly during her time at Facebook.

The duo met in late 2007 at a party. At the time, Facebook was not searching for a Chief Operations Officer officially, but Zuckerberg saw Sandberg as a perfect fit for the job. In 2008, Sandberg joined Facebook and began developing ways to make the company profitable. Before Sandberg joined Facebook, the company had only wanted to build a 'cool site'. The leadership assumed that profits would follow.

Sandberg changed this and by 2010, Facebook became profitable.

➢ Tony and Alfred (Zappos)

The combination of Tony Hsieh and Alfred Lin are a critical reason behind Zappos' undisputed success.

Hsieh was CEO, while Lin doubled as the COO and CFO, and their amazing work relationship helped scale Zappos into a billion-dollar company.

Zappos' culture was something that Hsieh was fully committed to, Lin supported this commitment, even when their board of directors elected to maximize profits at the cost of losing their culture.

When speaking about his working with Hsieh, Lin commented,

> *"I've worked with Tony for a long time. He doesn't like people saying 'no' to him. If you think it's a bad idea and you just say 'no,' it's really not a satisfying thing for anyone. And it's certainly not a satisfying thing for Tony. The best way to work with Tony is to help him refine his ideas as opposed to just saying 'no'".*

Lin left Zappos in 2010 to join the venture capital firm Sequoia Capital as a partner and that void is yet to be filled, till date.

It is important for every CEO to find a COO that he or she can work with, and vice versa. Some organizations don't understand the role of these two positions. In instances like this, there might be issues of power tussles.

But both positions are different and each is unique in its capacity. Both positions should be occupied by different classes of people.

How Can Visionaries and Operators Work Together?

Sometimes, issues and conflicts may arise between visionaries and operators. Conflicts may be aggravated if the roles of both positions are not clearly defined.

A visionary leader would give an organization a competitive advantage, while an operator provides the execution advantage. But if these positions and concepts are not understood, then there might not be an advantage for the company.

We have established that thinkers and doers are equally important, but the vision and direction will have to come from the visionary leader.

And since the direction for the company comes from the visionary leader a.k.a. the CEO, these closing sections of the chapter will focus on how the CEO can work with the operators of the company.

Some steps that can help with this include:

➢ Avoiding a Showdown of Egos at the Workplace

Visionary leaders need to know better than to show off, and treat all members of staff as equals and respect everyone. This way, the leader is very accessible and a member of the staff of the company does not feel any less than another.

➢ Develop a Dependable Hiring Process

Surround yourself with the right kind of people. Only people who understand the vision of the company and can work in line with it, should be brought in. This way, you can be sure that your staff will uphold your vision, even when you are not physically there.

➢ Mentoring and Coaching

Steps have to be taken to ensure that the junior ones learn the ropes of the company. This is why coming up with mentorship schemes is a hallmark of a company that wants to continue being successful in the decades to come.

➢ Integrating the Vision of Others

It is also important to note that new ideas may arise in the course of your work, and your company should find ways to integrate workable recommendations. Any beneficial advice from your staff can be worked into the overall vision of the company.

➢ **Persistence of Vision**

Leaders need to institutionalize a visionary framework to spread the vision in their company. This way, they can be sure their vision from the organization persists, even in their absence.

The Hallmark of a Visionary

The most notable challenge that visionaries face is not finding a worthy successor.

Successors of visionary leaders often have sizeable shoes to fill. And after a successor has taken on the role, it may seem like he or she is not doing a bad job, especially at the start. More so, if increased sales and profits are achieved.

But this is not enough.

Visionary companies are designed to prepare for the future. Making sales in the present is not a bad thing. But being able to create longevity for the future is a feature of visionary leaders. This is the defining trait that made leaders like Steve Jobs and Bill Gates stand out from other executives.

Sometimes, a visionary leader might need to be replaced within the organization. It is important that a person just as capable takes over.

Such a person guides the company towards a desirable future. This is the responsibility that visionary leaders face.

The way out of this would be hiring capable hands from the onset and mentoring these staff. This way, the organization will be in capable hands, in case there needs to be a change of leadership.

And to foster a satisfactory working relationship between all thinkers and doers of the company, we need to create a suitable place to work, and that's how we can guide the entire organization towards great and often unprecedented success.

All in All
(Learning Points)

- ✦ In running an organization, recognize that there are thinkers and there are doers.
- ✦ The thinkers are the visionaries while the doers are the operators.
- ✦ It is advised that the CEO of a company is a visionary while the COO is an operator.
- ✦ Both the visionary and operator are important in handling the affairs of the company.
- ✦ Efficient Visionary-Operator pairs have had positive effects on the growth of an organization.
- ✦ Visionary leaders should be on the lookout for the next generation of leaders and mentor them.

CHAPTER 12

Creating a Great Place to Work

Limelight No Longer

Some companies may seem on the surface, built to last forever.

They are constantly in the media spotlight...until they weren't. Ever wondered what happened to companies that were in the limelight till not too long ago?

Blockbuster was the largest DVD rental company in its heyday, but it filed for bankruptcy in 2010 due to internal feuds and their inability to adapt to technology.

Enron was a massive energy corporation that was worth billions, and its downfall in 2001 affected the lives of over 22,000 employees.

Other well-known multi-million-dollar brands that have filed for bankruptcy include Toys-R-Us, Pan American World Airways, and the international bookseller Borders.

In 2020 and beyond, 'big-name' brands today are more at risk of going out of business than ever.

Many of them seemed as if they would exist forever at the time but somehow, they have fallen into obscurity. And for most of these once household names, their downfall was most likely due to mismanagement.

Companies and organizations are like living things. They need basic 'nutrients' to survive and thrive in the harsh competitive environment most of these companies have to face. Many companies have perished over the years from not being well 'nourished' (in terms of company morale, effective leadership, and cash flow).

For a company to survive, it needs a competent management team that cares for the company and ensures it always gets everything that it needs to grow. The management team is also responsible for charting out the future course of the company. This way, not only is the present existence of the company protected, but the future is secured as well.

When a company has fallen into mismanagement, the damage may be repairable if it is discovered and corrected in time. With the right tools, a company on the path to failure due to bad management can be diagnosed and fixed.

Repairing damage is easier if problems are detected early, or better yet— prevented from happening.

An exemplary management team detects a problem early enough to prevent it. However, most management teams often only react to the problem after its occurrence.

When something is amiss in your company, one thing that a management team should focus on is company morale.

A well-managed company pays close attention to the morale of its employees. This should be a high priority, considering that morale affects employee performance. And employee performance determines the eventual profitability of the company.

Thus, a well-motivated workforce is very important in getting the most profitable results.

At Farrer Park Hospital and the other organizations I've been a part of, we understand this. This is why our management team has come up with practicable approaches that can diagnose and solve problems, even before they occur. This principle of a preemptive approach has saved us immeasurable amounts of time and money, as well as helping us to support a productive and successful working culture that is fulfilling and encouraging for our employees.

Some of our best approaches were developed with the help of a framework and profiling tool called the AEM Cube, and I want to share it with you here.

The Cube is an invaluable tool to help us harness the positive results that team diversity can bring, while managing potential downsides, so that your organization can endure and advance into the future without limits.

Getting the Best Outcomes with the AEM Cube

Most organizations exist in a competitive space.

Or as Charles Darwin puts it, it all comes down to the "survival of the fittest"—to survive in competitive spaces, you will require adaptability. But the 'fittest' or most successful organization in this context does not refer to the oldest or biggest companies. Neither does it refer to the companies with the highest revenues.

Being able to thrive requires organizational flexibility, and that is why the most successful organizations are the most flexible ones that can adapt to their operational environments. To achieve this flexibility, building and maintaining an effective team where diverse people can cooperate to achieve the company's goals is of critical importance.

This type of team can be created with the use of the AEM Cube. As a strategic tool in human resource management, it helps people understand their abilities and roles, both in the context of small teams or in the larger picture of the whole organization.

The AEM Cube does not only appraise the 'Visionary CEO'-to-'Operational COO' interaction, but also all other roles needed to execute a growth-curve for an organization, service, or product.

Developed by Professor Peter Robertson, a business consultant and psychiatrist, the Cube is built on the concepts of cybernetics, ethology, and complexity theory. The ethological concepts are based on the work of Nobel Prize laureates Konrad Lorenz and Niko Tinbergen.

Most importantly, it is a framework that can help you to build efficient teams by harnessing the benefits of team diversity, so that performance is maximized.

This happens by helping people understand the conditions under which they work best.

Using the AEM-Cube, members of your team can be assessed using questionnaires. The Cube assesses three aspects:

➢ **Attachment**

Attachment is the first dimension of the Cube that looks at how someone reacts to change or 'unknown factors' at work.

This dimension assesses if a person feels more secure to face the unknown due to strong relationships to people close to them, or having a strong emotional bond with the content of the task itself.

➢ Exploration

The second dimension of the AEM Cube defines how exploratory someone is.

Exploratory-oriented people tend to gather, analyse, and use the information from their environment—without knowing if the outcome is positive or not.

Stability-oriented people, on the other hand, prefer to make ideas concrete and then implement them accordingly. They are also interested in feedback that informs them how well or satisfactorily things are going.

➢ Complexity-Maturity

This dimension reveals the perspectives of individuals on a team; namely how well an individual has been able to use life experiences and develop abilities that are able to handle complex or unpredictable circumstances.

The "attachment" and "exploration" aspects form the base of the Cube, while the "complexity-maturity" aspect forms the vertical axis.

Teams are profiled using the individual values from the AEM assessment.

Once the data has been collated from the team and individual levels, the working styles and levels of diversity within a team are revealed, which allows for coaching steps for individual and team-wide improvement.

The AEM Cube can be used by business owners, CEOs, general managers, and HR managers to get the best outcomes from the workforce, irrespective of the level of diversity that exists in the team.

Many startups using the AEM Cube approach in managing their team from the very start, because the approach helps with getting the best people for the job, thereby improving the level of innovation and ability to get things done in your company.

Innovation and execution are key factors that improve the chances of survival and ultimate success of a company in a competitive environment, and the Cube can help with that.

The AEM Cube as a Pre-emptive Tool

A major advantage of using the AEM Cube is its usefulness as a preventive tool, which can help you to correct problems in your organization even before they happen.

And if you are already facing some problems with your workforce, the AEM Cube can serve as an amazing diagnostic tool to understand the issues so that you are better equipped to find resolution.

Whether you are currently facing an overt problem in your company or not, it is recommended that you leverage on the AEM Cube framework as early as possible. This way, you can prevent any potential problems with your staff even before they occur, even if everything is progressing at the moment.

In the organizations I've led, we understand the importance of using management tools like the AEM Cube to develop workable approaches to diagnosing and fixing problems.

Our results from using the AEM Cube include:

Improved performance—the Cube helps managers to understand each member of the team better and place them in areas where they would be most efficient.

Better alignment of the workforce towards organizational goals.

A higher level of adaptability of the company to change.

Higher chances of achieving team goals.

Improved hiring and HR decisions.

Higher effectiveness of development and training programmes.

Diversity in teams is better managed.

Let's go through how you can harness the unique advantages of diversity in the closing section of this chapter.

The Holistic Approach to Leadership

Most companies are made up of different people from varied cultural backgrounds. Apart from cultural diversity, there are also other forms of diversity in a company (gender, age, education, and so on).

This is why leaders in a company need to take a holistic approach to leadership.

A leader in a corporate environment is responsible for managing the diversity of a team and handling both simple and complex situations. He or she should also be able to come up with workable strategies that can leverage on the positive elements of diversity to achieve goals and help others work better with each other.

Harnessing the Strength in Diversity

Diversity leads to variability in the way individuals in your team process information.

Applied correctly, this can be a great advantage for a company seeking to reach out to a wide audience, because having a diverse team would help you understand the diverse groups of a large audience better.

The wider the audience, the wider the range of variability in your audience. This means that the more you listen to the different individuals in your team during your planning, the better off your strategies would be.

Each team member brings their unique perspective when deliberating on new ideas and methods. These perspectives are extremely important and effective when communicating to a particular class of your customer base.

As a leader, it is important to understand that the diversity of your team is one of its strengths, and not just another thing to be managed.

Diversity is only a weakness when not managed well.

Handling Efficient Communication

And speaking of managing weaknesses, one potential downside of having a diverse team is the increased risk of miscommunication.

A high level of diversity may lead to misunderstanding when ideas which are not expressed well enough, resulting in certain things not being well understood by some members of the team.

Working with a diverse team requires finding the most effective communication methods and the best channels to communicate with the team, especially when you are dealing with a large organization. Is it through a mobile app? Or does the traditional method of bulletin boards still remain relevant and effective?

In over thirty years of experience in the medical industry, I learned that a combination of both served my organizations most effectively to communicate to our diverse range of employees.

Good communication in a team is important in achieving an organization's goals.

Building Leaders for Tomorrow

Renowned American author and speaker, John C. Maxwell once tried to define a leader. He defined a leader as someone who:

"Knows the way, goes the way and shows the way".

The last part of this definition is vital to an organization's success. It is not enough for a leader to direct a team to achieve company goals—communicating and guiding them in a way that everyone understands is just as important.

An essential part of guiding your team is to create leaders that can speak for you and uphold your vision, in both smaller teams and larger departments.

That's why the leaders in a company should also prepare suitable members of the team to take up leadership positions.

There are five ways I've used to effectively prepare staff for leadership:

- **Vision-Casting**

A leader needs to share the grand vision of the company with his team members and help them identify with it. This way, the vision of the company becomes not just another piece of corporate talk, but something that's personal to individual members of the team. When done correctly, team members begin to see themselves as a part of something bigger than themselves, and are more committed and driven to achieve organizational goals.

- **Coaching**

As a leader, you should also share your knowledge and experiences with members of your team, especially the younger ones. This way, you help them grow faster because they can learn from your mistakes and improve on your successes.

- **Delegation**

Delegation is key to building leaders for tomorrow in your organization.

It is the skill of assigning responsibility to your staff - with the appropriate level of authority so that your assignees are empowered to execute to the best of their ability. Delegating responsibility isn't a 'drag and drop' task; it requires strategic supervision. As a leader, you are still responsible to guide your staff to achieve the desired end result. If you can delegate well, it is an effective method to give members of your team the experience and the capacity to become a leader.

➢ **Facilitating educational programmes**

Routine conferences and other educational programmes can be organized to instil leadership skills. For newer trainees, these programmes should cover actionable leadership lessons and management knowledge before moving on to advanced topics.

➢ **Encouraging networking within and outside your organization**

As a leader, it is important to help members of your team see the need to network. Apart from gaining new contacts, networking also improves communication skills. Having excellent communication skills is a must for leaders across all levels.

In order to find out which staff members have the greatest propensity for leadership, you'll need to have a high level of interaction with the people in your team—which allows you to understand the personality traits of these individuals and discover more about them.

To help your future leaders improve, either you or your key management staff can also make personal recommendations to guide them on an individual level.

If you can use management tools to solve existing issues, pre-empt future problems, and effectively harness the diversity within your workforce, then you will be on track to creating an acceptable place for your employees to work, establishing leaders at all levels of your company, and ensuring long-lasting enduring success for your company.

When you have a happy workforce, never-before-seen results are sure to follow. In the next chapter, we'll be going in-depth into what it looks like when companies get it right.

All in All
(Learning Points)

- Good management pays close attention to the morale of its employees and aims to solve a problem before it occurs—it's the secret to standing the test of time as a company.
- AEM Cube is great as a diagnostic tool for your workforce to optimize the best outcomes from your team.
- Diversity in your teams can be a decided advantage for a company that seeks to reach out to a wide audience, because having a diverse team would help you understand a diverse audience better.
- The diversity of a team should be its strength, not its weakness. To handle diverse teams, holistic leadership that takes all factors into account is required.
- A good leader cares about building leaders for tomorrow by preempting future problems, effectively harnessing the diversity within your workforce, and using management tools to solve existing issues.

CHAPTER 13

Motivating People the Right Way

It Starts with a Happy Workforce

Globally recognized for a wide range of computer products and related services, Microsoft is one of the biggest tech companies in the world. On April 25, 2019, the company exceeded a trillion dollars in market valuation.

This made Microsoft the third tech company after Apple and Amazon to achieve this feat. Microsoft also ranked No. 30 in the list of largest United States corporations, as compiled by Fortune 500.

But they couldn't have done it without guiding and taking care of their people.

Most people don't realize that Microsoft also ranks highly in 'Best Places to Work' lists. The Chief Diversity Officer of Microsoft, Lindsay-Rae McIntyre mentioned the strong commitment of the company to foster a culture of inclusion for all of its employees.

McIntyre commented that they've,

> *"deepened our commitment to building a more inclusive environment through programs like unconscious bias training, expanded parental leave, immersive experiences like Dialogues Across Differences, and the continued support for the growth of our eight Employee Resource Groups and 40 Employee Networks."*

Zoom Video Communications is another company that's also commonly indexed as one of the 'Best Places To Work'.

A top account executive of the company gave excellent remarks about the company in an interview. He said this about the company,

> *"Fantastic company culture of 'Happiness.' You feel it every day and you can't wait to come to work because you feel cared for."*

That's why staff motivation and work satisfaction is so important in an organization.

To achieve the goals of the company, you need a workforce that is prepared to go all out for the company. Every employee should be excited about the value of their work and the position they occupy within the organization, and look forward to new challenges and opportunities to learn.

Since motivated employees perform better and achieve more than employees who are not, it's important to find efficient methods to keep your staff motivated and inspired.

After all, there is no such thing as status quo in business. Your company either grows and advances into the future with a driven and purposeful workforce, or it loses touch and falls into obscurity as employees find no reason to do anything more than the regular routine.

It is important to understand motivation frameworks and how they can help you to understand and maximize the performance of your employees—that's what we'll be covering in this chapter.

The following sections will guide you in finding the best strategies to keep your employees motivated.

Motivational Frameworks

➢ Maslow's Hierarchy of Needs

You may have heard it before—Abraham Maslow's Hierarchy of Needs is one of the most popular frameworks in psychology and employee motivation.

Maslow proposed the idea first in 1943, stating that motivation is the result of a person's attempt to meet five basic needs:

- Physiological
- Safety
- Social
- Esteem
- Self-actualization

According to this framework, these needs affect the behaviour of people and are important in their motivation. And your employees are people, too—at different levels of needs. Understanding and satisfying their needs goes a long way in employee motivation.

Physiological needs are needs required for human survival, e.g. food, water, and sleep. As a manager, it may not be obvious but you should ensure that the physiological needs of your employees at work are taken care of. Providing comfortable working conditions and reasonable work schedules helps achieve this. This way, you allow employees enough time to get the necessary rest and nutrition.

That's why the larger companies, especially those in the tech industry, provide free meals and even a place to sleep overnight so that they can care for their staff. Even from a purely commercial standpoint, it makes sense to provide physiological requirements because the economic benefits of your staff being able to worry less on such matters and focus more on productive work far outweigh the cost.

However, in order to save costs, some companies cut down on these basic needs. If your employees are having trouble fulfilling these needs, that's taking away the time, effort, and focus that they could have spent on furthering your company's goals.

In the next level of Maslow's hierarchy is safety needs, which includes providing employees with a sense of security and well-being. Ensuring job security and secure compensation are great ways to start fulfilling employees' safety needs—paying them late will only serve to make them wary and is likely to reduce their performance.

All humans have a primal need to feel a sense of belonging and acceptance in social circles. Most employees don't work well in isolation.

This is why it is important to create a warm ambience in your organization to meet the third level of Maslow's hierarchical framework: social needs.

Social needs of your employees are met when they feel that they are part of something bigger than themselves, and building smaller teams within your company is an efficient way to cater to these needs. As a leader, your employees need to feel that you are accessible.

The fourth and second-highest need is Esteem, and you can care for this with recognition and appreciation initiatives, such as promotions, bonuses, awards, and gifts.

The final need is far more personal: Self-actualization. It describes a person's need to reach his or her full potential. Providing employees with new challenges that are attainable yet demanding can help meet selfactualization needs and allow them to grow to their fullest abilities.

If you want to assess how well you are taking care of your staff, frameworks like Maslow and his Hierarchy of Needs are a great place to start!

McClelland's Human Motivation Theory

The Human Motivation Theory by David McClelland is another framework that defines and helps leaders to motivate their employees. In this model, McClelland identified three motivators that he believed were present in everyone.

- The Need for Achievement
- The Need for Affiliation
- The Need for Power

People can be classified based on their dominant motivator. To keep a person motivated, you would have to find out their dominant motivator and meet that need.

The dominant motivator depends, to a large extent, on our culture and life experiences and each dominant motivator tells you the unique features of the people who are motivated by it.

Here's a quick guide on these motivators:

People with a dominant need for achievement:

- take calculated risks
- have a strong need to set up and meet with challenging goals
- enjoy working alone
- like to receive regular feedback on their progress and achievements

- People with a dominant need for affiliation:
- want to belong to groups
- prefer collaboration to competition
- do not like uncertainty
- want to be liked, and will often go along with the choice of the majority

People with a dominant need for power:

- enjoy status and recognition
- like to control and influence others
- always want to win arguments
- enjoy competition and winning

Your employees will fall under these three classes, and the first thing you will need to do is to classify employees based on their motivators. Roles and responsibilities can then be assigned based on their strengths and weaknesses.

For instance, people with the need for achievement like to handle new challenges and are good candidates to spearhead new projects.

Power-dominant people may be a good fit for sales and certain leadership positions, while people with the need for affiliation should not be assigned to high-risk projects. This is because they prefer stability and do not appreciate risks - leave it to the ones who do! They can be motivated without extra money by giving them more control over their work, resources, and other employees.

Herzberg's Two-Factor Theory

Frederick Herzberg developed this theory in 1959 with much empirical evidence to confirm its validity.

His framework is simple; it states that job satisfaction depends on two kinds of factors: satisfaction and dissatisfaction factors.

The satisfaction factors are referred to as motivators (not to be confused with McClelland's motivators), while the dissatisfaction factors are termed as hygiene factors, all of which act independently of each other.

The motivators include individual performance, responsibility, job status and available opportunities for growth.

The hygiene factors include salary, relationship with colleagues, work environment, and relationships with superiors.

If you are aiming to reduce dissatisfaction from your work environment, removing hygiene factors should be your priority. But reducing dissatisfaction is only one-half of Herzberg's framework. To increase job satisfaction and achieve greater performance from your staff, you will need to add more motivators to the organization.

Your staff may respond differently to different motivation strategies, so be flexible in finding the best framework to keep your staff motivated.

As a member of the key management of different organizations, we understand this need for flexibility in keeping staff motivated. Some of our approaches to finding the best framework to use in motivating staff are highlighted in this chapter. Not all motivation frameworks can work in all kinds of companies.

In some instances, you might need to combine two or more frameworks to achieve results, or modify an existing framework to suit your company.

At the beginning of the chapter, we briefly talked about how companies like Microsoft and Zoom Communications did well when it comes to employee motivation. Let's delve a little deeper into actual instances of employee motivation done right.

Happy Staff, Happy Results

➢ Google

Google is one of the top brands to consider when it comes to employee motivation, especially during the years where they won awards for their efforts and were the go-to company when it came to employee engagement and satisfaction.

The 50,000 strong company was named "Best Company to Work For" in 2014 by Fortune Magazine and the Great Place to Work Institute, and they have made the top ranks of many other indexes since then.

What is even more amazing is the 6-star treatment Google gives its employees. This has helped the company get unique and outstanding contributions from these employees.

Google's motivation strategies have proven to be highly efficient at producing stellar results. Ironically, companies that focused on producing results end up failing - Google succeeded because they focused on the people.

The company's work philosophy is,

"To create the happiest, most productive workplace in the world."

The words from the Vice President of People Development for the company only corroborates this philosophy:

"It's less about the aspiration to be No. 1 in the world, and more that we want our employees and future employees to love it here, because that's what's going to make us successful."

Another interesting thing to note about the Google approach to motivation is the fact that it is surprisingly cost-efficient. The company uses many uncommon, yet affordable perks to motivate employees, and they are not afraid to go to extreme lengths to keep employees happy.

Google offers employees other extrinsic benefits apart from basic remuneration. These benefits include flexible spending accounts, insurance, vacation packages, and tuition reimbursements.

Apart from the perks of working at Google, the company makes concerted efforts to create an amazing work environment for employees.

Some of the added benefits Googlers enjoy include:

- Fully paid parental benefits for new parents
- Reimbursement of up to $5,000 to cater to legal expenses
- Financial support for employees who want to adopt a child with Google's Adoption Assistance
- Onsite mechanical garage (for car and bike maintenance) and spa at the company headquarters
- Onsite doctor, fitness centre, and laundromat which are free for Google staff at the Googleplex
- Free lunches and dinners for Google staff

Google offers a holistic approach to employee motivation, where every staff member has a voice and is given a sense of belonging in running the company's affairs.

The company hosts an employee forum every Friday where the 20 most asked questions are answered. This way, employees can use several channels to communicate their ideas and thoughts.

Employees can communicate directly with Google leaders via emails, and timely feedback about managers are also collated. Results from surveys are used to run a public acknowledgement of the best managers. The lower performing managers, on the other hand, are provided with more support and coaching.

➢ Netflix

Founded in 1997, Netflix is also popular for offering employees juicy perks and privileges.

One of the most popular perks Netflix offers its employees is the extended parental leave. The company offers employees a whole year of paid leave when they have children (either by birth or adoption).

This is almost triple what most other companies give as parental leave. Netflix does this in support of new parents. The extended parental leave helps new parents get enough rest and recovery.

This way, they can offer their best when they return.

- **In-N-Out Burger**

In-N-Out Burger is another company that has managed to stay in the 'Best Companies to Work For' list for a while.

Unlike other companies, In-N-Out Burger does not offer many perks outside the basic pay, but the burger company pays its employees very well.

Store managers with In-N-Out Burger can earn as much as over $160,000, more than what the typical tech worker earns per annum. The high wages for fast-food workers have positive effects on the company, namely improved productivity, reduced employee turnover and more profits in the long run.

Interestingly enough, In-N-Out Burger does not require high qualifications to get in.

- **Bain and Company**

Bain and Company is a global management consulting firm, with the company headquarters situated in Boston. The company has also been listed as one of the best companies to work for.

What makes Bain and Company a great place to work is the comprehensive benefits programme of the company. The programme includes a great health insurance plan, considerate parental leave packages, vacations and paid time off, and a generous retirement plan.

Apart from the basic perks, the company offers tuition assistance, paid time to get into volunteer work, diversity and job training programmes, plus sabbatical and remote working options.

What These Companies Are Getting Right

The high praises these companies get from employees are a telling indicator that they are using the right motivation strategies.

And to ensure that your motivational strategies are built on the right foundation, check that your frameworks are centred on people and not solely on outcomes.

Humans are not machines—you'll have to consider the emotional and physiological state of your employees in relation to their work.

But it is not enough to simply find the perfect framework for your company.

You must also understand the best way to *implement* the selected framework. For instance, some motivational frameworks require adding special bonuses for staff. It is important to define the clear conditions under which these bonuses are to be earned. Where public appreciation methods are used to motivate staff, the appreciation schemes should be fully transparent.

For example, if an 'Employee of the Month' is to be selected 12 times a year, the selection process should be fair and easily understood by everyone.

This way, all employees are aware of the selection criteria.

Some important points for the optimal implementation of a motivational framework in your company include:

➢ **Transparency**

It is important to ensure transparency when implementing a motivation strategy. This way, all members of staff are aligned and invested to participate fully in the process.

➢ Flexibility

A satisfactory level of flexibility is also required for implementing motivation strategies. Some strategies might not show immediate results. Managers should be able to adjust the necessary variables to get the best outcomes from a motivation strategy.

➢ Futuristic Thinking

In implementing a motivational framework in your company, you should ensure that it is sustainable in the years to come.

This way, you can be sure that the result of the framework is not just a one-off thing, but a sustainable strategy that will propel your company into the success that others can only dream of.

At the end of the day, having happy employees would help you save in costs - much, much more than you will expect (in employee turnover, training, legal fees, and other expenses) and reap more profits for you in the long run.

Efficient motivational frameworks keep your employees happy with their jobs, which is the only way staff can be fully committed to the goals of the company.

In the final chapter, we will wrap everything up with company culture.

After all, "culture eats strategy for breakfast"—first said by Peter Drucker and later made famous by Mark Fields, President at Ford.

All in All
(Learning Points)

- ✦ Motivation requires understanding and satisfying the needs of your staff.
- ✦ Humans have physical, social and emotional needs, and happy people produce the best results.

- Different motivation frameworks work for different organizations, and finding the perfect motivational framework for your organization requires flexibility. To achieve success in motivating your employees, transparency is pivotal in implementing a motivational framework.
- The right motivation strategy is incomplete without the right implementation. To complete your efforts, your employee motivation strategy should be centred on people, not just on outcomes.

CHAPTER **14** ►►►

Culture Drives the Company

An Inspirational Future

We've discussed time and again the importance of engaged and empowered staff. As masses of millennials join the workforce (and the ranks of your company), the ability of your leaders to engage employees is of greater importance than ever before.

Where do your employees see themselves in the next 5, or even 10 years?

The young people in your company need to see a future with your company.

We know that some of their strengths are learning, adapting, using technology with a natural ease - and when empowered, they are able to maximize their gifts and contribute to the success of your company.

That's why an inspiring culture is the key to developing high-performing employees.

At Farrer Park Hospital, our culture is our single biggest secret that contributes more to our success than any strategy, tactic, or plan.

Rather than place too much emphasis on operations, finance, or strategy, we realize that our people are our most valuable asset. That's why our energies are focused on culture, staff engagement, communication with employees, and service initiatives.

This chapter is about how we managed to create and support an inspiring, high-performance culture that has enabled us to achieve the status of an award-winning hospital despite only opening recently in 2016.

Empowered to Lead, Guide and Adapt

In the past several years, we've mentored Heads of Departments and team members to lead, guide, and make critical decisions at Farrer Park Hospital, despite many of them being very young.

We implemented Cross-Functional Training (CFT) as a synergistic approach for employees to understand and appreciate the diligence and challenges of other teams.

By understanding job scopes that are out of their own, their competencies and abilities are raised. We've not only got them to appreciate other seemingly disparate team members in the organization through CFT, but also to be able to see more avenues for solutions and think on their feet with this kind of exposure.

In Chapter Nine, we talked about cross-attachment training outside the company, and how companies can experience a massive uplift in employee capability.

Cross-Functional Training is the *internal implementation* of this principle, where we cross-train our staff internally.

On a personal level, our young employees go through a structured three-year personalized training road map called the Individual Development Plan.

This plan allows us to implement training that upgrades their individual skill sets. The benefit of this training on a consistent basis empowers them with career mobility and an enriching experience as a member of Farrer Park Hospital.

Previously, we've also discussed how assessment and profiling tools can be of great benefit to engaging and improving your workforce (Chapter Twelve). We too, use the AEM Cube to help us identify and analyse an individual's maximum performance and potential.

From helping us discern which new recruits are the best fit in the hospital to aligning the entire organization towards our collective vision, Farrer Park Hospital gained the ability to reassign roles and responsibilities to maximize their potential and the hospital's overall aptitude.

The key management executives of the hospital are sent for consulting sessions that evaluate their strategic leadership and discover the best approaches to working with them.

All team leaders are also required to attend a one-and-a-half-day 'The Power Of One' team building programme (discussed previously when we talked about increasing staff satisfaction in Chapter Four).

Here, we align their personal values with the Vision, Mission, and Core Values of Farrer Park Hospital. We help them understand team development roles and dynamics, and recognize their personal team leadership styles.

After understanding and recognizing these concepts, we will go into identifying factors that contribute to successful teamwork and ultimately develop a plan to achieve our organization's goals.

Our training does not stop at assessment and profiling. In order to raise our standards for service excellence, we continue to train our staff with customized programmes to impart and instil the Farrer Service Mindset.

The Farrer Service Mindset programme was set up to allow our hospital staff to discover their value in their personal lives and the healthcare industry at large. They will also be able to see the importance of their own unit as a contributing component to Farrer Park Hospital's vision.

Employees who participated in this programme acquired the skills to build rapport with patients, patients' families, and doctors. One of the most important skills imparted is the ability to deliver consistent service through positive service language and the highly underrated skill of proactive listening.

When these skills are put together in a team effort, a remarkable and consistently memorable customer experience is the result.

Our employees are empowered to go the extra mile and continually add value to our patients - but that's not all!

As most of our employees are customer-facing, they have to look as presentable to our patients to complete the entire experience.

With our Professional Image Programme, all members of Farrer Park Hospital can be depended upon to project a professional appearance that projects presence, confidence, power, and poise.

Professional hair-styling and make-up is a core part of this programme, but our staff are also trained in stance, eye contact, hand placement, and even a professional handshake.

People may not expect nurses, patient care technicians, and other hospital staff to possess a polished professional demeanour like they would to a flight attendant or a hotel receptionist, but that doesn't mean we should take it easy.

Just as how we make the effort to go the additional mile for our patients, we'll make the same effort for our personal presentation.

It may not seem like something significant, but the results and accolades speak for themselves - have a look below.

Achieved: Service Excellence

CLINICAL EXCELLENCE

Global Health and Travel Awards 2018:
Cardiology Service Provider of the Year in Asia Pacific

Icons of Healthcare:
Leading Hospital for Cardiovascular Care

Global Health and Travel Awards 2017:
Oncology Service Provider of the Year

EMPLOYEE ENGAGEMENT AND DEVELOPMENT

The Singapore HR Awards 2017:
Employee Engagement and Alignment and Using Digital Media in HR. Recruitment and Selection and Workplace Safety and Health

HRM Awards 2017:
Best HR Transformation Through Technology

HRD Asia Hot List 2018

CMO Asia: CEO of the Year 2017. 50 Most Talented Healthcare Leaders of Asia 2016

Singapore Business Management Excellence Awards 2016: Employee Engagement of the Year - Health Products and Services

Asian Hospital Management Awards 2017:
Talent Development

Human Resources Asia Recruitment Awards 2017:
Best Recruitment Evaluation Technique

The Golden Globe Tigers 2017:
Excellence in Training and Development

LinkedIn Power profiles 2017:
Most Viewed CEOs on LinkedIn in Singapore 2017

TECHNOLOGY AND INNOVATION

Global Health and Travel Awards 2018:
Smart Hospital of the Year in Asia Pacific 2017 and 2018

Hospital Management Asia Pacific Awards 2017:
Excellence in Disruptive Technologies

Asian Hospital Management Awards 2016: Marketing, PR or Online Presence. Innovations in Healthcare IT

Enterprise Innovation Awards 2017:
Enterprice Innovators - Healthcare 2016 & 2017

Healthcare & Pharmaceutical Leading Experts Awards 2016:
Healthcare & Pharmaceutical Leading Experts Awards

OPERATIONS AND SERVICE EXCELLENCE

Singapore Health Quality Service Awards
2019: 1 Gold and 44 Silver Award Winners
2018: 2 Gold and 37 Silver Award Winners

CIO Advisor Top 10 APAC Startups in Healthcare 2017

Icons of Healthcare:
Best Integrated Healthcare and Wellness Complex

Frost and Sullivan Asia Pacific 2017 Best Practices Awards:
2017 Asia Pacific Hospital of the Year in Patient Experience

National Arts Council Singapore: Friend of the Arts

Human Resouces HR Vendors of the Year 2017:
Best Corporate Healthcare Provider

Global Health and Travel 2016:
Best New Hospital of the Year in Asia Pacific

5th Eldercare Innovation Awards 2017:
Best Home Care Operator and Best Hospitality of Care

BCA Green Mark: BCA Green Mark Platinum

None of the above could have been achieved without the culture that we've built together at Farrer Park Hospital.

We have seen the meteoric rise of companies over the years... and the equally abrupt fall from grace for some of them. A supersonic growth must be supported by a strong culture, no matter how solid the business strategy.

While companies like Apple and Southwest Airlines have held fast through many difficult times, others have given way into obscurity.

At Farrer Park Hospital, we don't take our current success for granted—we tirelessly work to maintain and improve the culture and infrastructure we've built over the years.

To play my part, I take time from my duties to deliver a series of CEO's Weekly Motivational Messages to inspire and encourage my employees to achieve their goals.

In these messages, I focus on what is best for them and what they need to hear. It is all about them and the plan for their career and continued progression with us.

Constant communication through messages like these are encouraging, but nothing can replace personal interaction - and that's why once a week, I make the time to meet face-to-face with a small group of employees to hear them out and listen carefully to their feedback and suggestions.

These motivational messages and coffee sessions are the personal touches that I take to empower and motivate my employees, which we've already spoken at length in Chapter Four. However, I cannot stress enough the importance of taking care of your staff so that they can take care of your customers (or patients in the case of Farrer Park Hospital).

Leading the Culture with Leadership 4.0

Our training programmes for the employees and team leader of Farrer Park Hospital set the groundwork for a strong, high-performing culture.

But it's not enough.

We need to embrace the evolving dynamics of the Fourth Industrial Revolution with a different and more adaptive style of understanding and leadership.

To put the idea of industrial revolutions into context:

The First Industrial Revolution started with the mechanization and invention of the steam engine (18th century).

The second was brought about by production lines that were launched by Henry Ford's automotive factories (19th century).

The third was when the proliferation of electronics in telecommunications and computers became mainstream, giving rise to automation and robotics (20th century).

Today, the Fourth Industrial Revolution is the cyber-physical systems that resulted in the full integration and connectivity with computers, networking devices, and cloud networks.

One thing that's of no doubt about the industrial changes happening today is that the interactions between individuals, small companies, and large enterprises will be different.

The way we conduct business and talk to each other will never be the same. Just like how the internet has dramatically changed the entire world, our environment will soon see the impact of disruptive technologies and trends such as the Internet of Things (IoT), virtual reality (VR), and artificial intelligence (AI).

This means that our priorities need to evolve as well.

In the industrial age (18th - 20th centuries), companies tend to focus in this order: Profit as the first priority, followed by Product, Quality, People and lastly Recycling.

In the digital age today, the most successful companies are the ones that prioritize People first, followed by Quality, Recycling, Product, and lastly Profit.

Successful leaders understand that profit comes naturally and in larger quantities when you focus your priority in the order where People come first.

That's why employee engagement is so important.

To lead in today's Industry 4.0, we need to engage with an active leadership. But what does it mean to have an active CEO and management?

It means that we need to lead with the four factors of Leadership 4.0:

➢ 1. Authenticity

- In a world where anyone can claim just about anything on the Internet with photoshopped profile pictures and fake news, authenticity and "being real" is a premium that few people get right.
- As a leader, we may feel that we need to present a certain persona to our employees, but we may not realize that they know if we're coming across as authentic or if we're just putting on an act.

➢ 2. Empathy

- With the world progressing at breakneck pace, it's easy to focus solely on information and forget about the experiences and feelings of other people.
- We need to show care for our customers and employees, and know how other people are interacting with your brand (products, services, experience, speed of work, and tools they are using).

➢ 3. Over-Communication

- It's far better to get the message and risk communicating a little too much rather than to hint and lose the meaning you're looking to get across.
- I've found that anything worth communicating is often undercommunicated.
- That's why rather than saying too little, we need to over-communicate.

➢ 4. Trust

- Your stakeholders (customers and employees) are looking for a company that they can trust.

- How reliable is your company? Can a customer trust the promise of your brand to deliver? If your company is perceived as reliable and trustworthy, your success is only capped by your imagination, and the sky's the limit.

If we are able to implement these four factors of Leadership 4.0 into how we lead and manage our companies, we can achieve organizational success.

And here's how I would like to define organizational success: If we take care of our staff, they can take care of our customers and our organization.

It's a principle that's close to my heart and you've read it more than once in this book, but I cannot stress enough. Your employees are your 'internal customers'; treat them like your customers and that's how you take care of employees.

Some companies are surprised to learn that their customers actually care about how you treat your employees. It's related to authenticity.

If you treat your customers well and your employees poorly, word gets around. And the thing you'll lose is authenticity. When authenticity goes down, it's likely that trust and revenue will follow in short order.

To keep your company on the upward trend to success, remember the four factors of Leadership 4.0 and your goals will be closer than you think!

My name is Dr. Timothy Low and thank you for accompanying me on this written expedition on employee engagement and workplace satisfaction. I hope the words here help you find your way and triangulate your path to success, and that you will take advantage of all the knowledge I've shared so that you too, can be the leader that your people need.

All in All
(Learning Points)

- An inspiring culture is the key to developing high-performing employees.
- A company's supersonic growth must be supported by a strong culture, no matter how solid the business strategy.
- Rather than place too much emphasis on operations, finance, or strategy, we realize that our people are our most valuable asset.

Epilogue

Leadership today is far different from what it was just two decades ago. Back then, just merely holding the title of a leader was enough to accomplish your goals. Today, this form of "armchair leadership" is not sufficient, effective, or appreciated.

Companies around the world have also observed that leading their employees requires more than just instructions from the top and a system for them to follow.

To cope, many of them have incorporated technology to expedite their processes and stay relevant in a digital world where change is accelerating faster than ever.

But more technology is not what people need, per se. Rather, we need to use 'high-tech' to nurture 'high-touch'. This means that we need to focus on making an emotional impact on our employees and our customers. We need to work on "emotional-selling", rather than traditional "hard-selling".

CEOs and organizational leaders need to practise using not just their heads, but their hearts and hands as well. In order to successfully support our head-based planning, we need to use our hearts to care for our staff and use our hands to guide our people (this is what I talked about in Leadership 4.0).

In today's Industry 4.0 climate, it's necessary to be a 4.0 Leader.

When I was thrust into my first leadership position, it wasn't something

I desired at first. I was always an apt follower; following up with clear and constant communication so that my superiors are always kept in the loop.

As a first-time CEO in 2000, I kept up the same communication style - to my management staff and employees. I listened hard to what was happening on the ground so that I can feel the real challenges, subsequently creating an empathetic and encouraging place to work in.

Back then, I wasn't thinking about terms like 'Leadership 4.0', but my leadership style was that of a highly active CEO, where I would be communicating the vision, quarterly mission, and weekly agendas using different channels.

After all, if it's worth communicating, then it's worth overcommunicating!

To some, I may appear to have achieved a lot, but leadership isn't a destination. It's always fluid. A perpetual journey, if you will.

You can't just have a one-size-fits-all framework for every company you lead.

When I tried to use the previous success from one hospital to another, I quickly learned that different companies had cultures that were as contrasting as night and day.

Just like how I had to adjust and accommodate the different cultures of various hospitals and organizations that I lead, you are likely to find that it's never the same. We constantly need to adapt to new industries, diversified communities, the ever-changing times, evolving social norms, and especially the next generation.

And part of this perpetual journey means that I'm constantly learning and adding to my "war chest" of frameworks so I can integrate them into my leadership approaches.

I'm not yet at a place where I've arrived, and I always ask myself this:

Would my employees choose me to be their leader if they had a choice?

If you put yourself in their shoes, mentality, and present circumstances, would you choose yourself to be your leader?

We rarely get to choose our leaders, but would you rather be the type of leader that your employees feel "forced" to follow or one whose leadership they would gladly choose, no matter how difficult the task ahead?

For those that I've had the opportunity to lead, it's my privilege to say that most would follow me if they had the choice to.

Not because of any coercion or strong-arm tactic, but because I would take the time to communicate with them. To find common ground with them. And most importantly, to empathize and guide them to a better future together with the company.

Each and every one of them will always be given the chance to grow as a leader too.

At every level of the organization, I build leaders so that they can, in turn, build more leaders. By touching lives, making a difference to them, and building leaders that can lead others.

In today's business landscape, our employees need this form of leadership more than ever. It's been the secret of successful companies that have stood the test of time, and it can be your greatest tool in your leadership kit.

Another way to call it would be 'distributed leadership', where power is shared across the organization rather than being concentrated in only a few people in many traditional companies.

In many companies, many unsolved problems occur as a result of only one person holding on to power. By empowering employees with leadership ability and increasing their autonomy, modern organizations using this leadership style can result in collective solutions when everyone in the company works together collaboratively.

If you want your company to maintain high-quality standards in the face of competition and evolving technology, you will need to create a culture that can preserve a healthy ecosystem.

In today's environment, we need our employees to be adaptable and quick to react to change, while staying passionate about their work. That's how to have an engaged workforce that's fully involved and empowered to perform.

In order to create such a culture, the leader needs the defining skill set of emotional intelligence, or 'emotelligence'. Others will want to follow a leader with high emotional intelligence because this type of leadership tends to be more skilled in decision-making, managing relationships, and work performance.

Such leaders exhibit qualities like empathy, patience, kindness, and forgiveness amongst others.

After sharing with you my life's work and experiences in this book, my message really comes down to this:

With high emotional intelligence, you'll succeed where others fail.

And you'll be the leader that others want to follow.

If you found the leadership lessons in this book inspiring, please share it with someone you want to inspire.

Index

Chapter One: "Conventional Wisdom"

Chapter Two: The Alternative: 6-Star Success

Genius Bar

Golden Globe Awards

HBO

Irving Berlin

NPD Group, Inc

Plies

Puttin' on the Ritz

Ritz-Carlton

Jobs, Steve

The Diamond as Big as the Ritz

Ritz-Carlton

Ritz-Carlton Leadership Centre

The Trumpet of the Swan

White, E.B.

Chapter Three: "Serving Inside" First

Apple

David Dao

DreamWorks Animation

Farrer Park Hospital

Full Contact

Gallup

How To Train Your Dragon

Kung-Fu Panda

Mocsoy, Steve

Shrek

Southwest Airlines

Chapter Four: Inside-Out Approach

Chapter Five: Serving from the Heart

Glassdoor

Global Health and Travel Magazine

- Best New Hospital of the Year in Asia Pacific

Gone in Sixty Seconds

Hospital Management Asia

- Asian Hospital Management Award

Human Resources Magazine

- Asia Recruitment Awards
- Best Recruitment Evaluation Technique
- Human Resources Magazine Awards
- Special Recognition for Best HR Transformation Through Technology

Management Excellence Award

Mustang

Netflix

Nicholas Cage

Pandora

Questex

Ritz-Carlton

Singapore Business Review

- Employee Engagement of the Year

Southwest Airlines

Chapter Six: How to Put Excellence into Service

Amazon

Apple

Christensen, John

Disneyland

Chapter Seven: It Doesn't Mean You Need a Big Budget...

Chapter Eight: But Spare No Expense for the Customer

Tim Manners

Vicky Chase

Chapter 9: Learning from the Best

Chartered Institute of Personnel and Development

Farrer Park Hospital

Irish Post Office

Lee Kong Chian School of Medicine

McDonald's

Ms. Lim

Nanyang Technological University

Peace River Pulp

Ritz-Carlton

UK Institute of Practitioners

Chapter Ten: Giving Back

Abbott Medical Optics

Au Eong, Kah Guan

Bausch and Lomb

CarMax

Cheng, Bobby

Cone Communications

Equinox

Farrer Park Hospital

Greenpac

Lee Kong Chian School of Medicine

Chapter Eleven: Every Visionary Needs an Operator

Time Magazine

Wozniak, Steve

Yahoo

Zappos

Zuckerberg, Mark

Chapter Twelve: Creating a Great Place to Work

AEM Cube

Blockbuster

Borders

Darwin, Charles

Enron

Farrer Park Hospital

Maxwell, John C.

Pan American World Airways

Robertson, Peter

Toys-R-Us

Chapter Thirteen: Motivating People the Right Way

Amazon

Apple

Bain and Company

Drucker, Peter

Fields, Mark

Fortune 500

Fortune Magazine

Chapter Fourteen: Culture Drives the Company

"People don't care how much you know until they know how much you care."

– Theodore Roosevelt

TRIANGULATION OF SUCCESS

Value Creation for employees, customers & shareholders